London's Waterside Walks

London's Waterside Walks

Brian Cookson

MAINSTREAM
PUBLISHING

EDINBURGH AND LONDON

Dedicated to Susan

First published in Great Britain in 2004 by
MAINSTREAM PUBLISHING COMPANY (EDINBURGH) LTD
7 Albany Street
Edinburgh EH1 3UG

ISBN 1 84018 808 1

A catalogue record for this book
is available from the British Library

Typeset in Times New Roman and Univers

Printed and bound in Great Britain by
The Bath Press Ltd

ACKNOWLEDGEMENTS

I have been helped in my researches for the book by many people, including local societies, authors of books, Blue Badge educators and several Blue Badge tourist guides. I would also like to pay tribute to the City Literary Institute who employed me to develop and run the courses which resulted in the guided walks described in this book. Above all I am grateful to my wife, Susan, who has advised me on all aspects of the book and provided several of the photographs, and to my daughter, Sarah, whose sharp eyes have considerably improved the text.

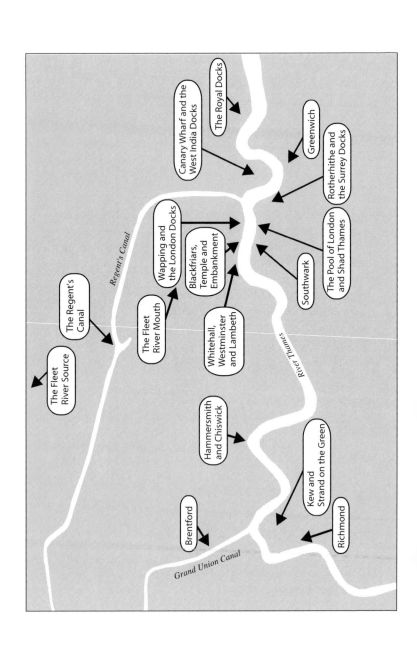

The Fleet River Source

The Regent's Canal

Regent's Canal

The Fleet River Mouth

Wapping and the London Docks

Blackfriars, Temple and Embankment

Whitehall, Westminster and Lambeth

Canary Wharf and the West India Docks

The Royal Docks

Greenwich

Rotherhithe and the Surrey Docks

The Pool of London and Shad Thames

Southwark

River Thames

Hammersmith and Chiswick

Kew and Strand on the Green

Richmond

Brentford

Grand Union Canal

CONTENTS

PREFACE

There is no more enjoyable way to explore London than to walk along its various waterways. The walker is rewarded with world-famous historic views such as the Houses of Parliament and Tower Bridge, as well as exciting, modern waterside developments along the regenerated South Bank and Docklands. Over the last few years, the Thames Path has been opened up as far downstream as the Barrier, and the canals and former docks given a new lease of life. We can therefore now visit waterside areas which in the past were unsafe or completely inaccessible.

Whilst working as a London Blue Badge guide, I have realised how important the Thames is to London's history and present development, and how much visitors thrill at the views along the river.

The walks were developed for the London Walks courses run for the City Literary Institute. During the six years I have been running these courses I have guided hundreds of people on these walks along the Thames and its surrounding docks and canals. The walks have been selected for their historic, cultural and scenic interest and can roughly be divided into four groups – the Thames itself (central and outer London), the canals, Docklands and the 'hidden rivers'. Each walk covers about two to three miles on foot, although I occasionally suggest using a bus, the Underground or Docklands Light Railway to cover longer distances between points of interest. At a leisurely pace and taking time to study the area and enjoy the views, the walks are designed to last about two hours. They will of course take longer if you yield to the temptation to stop at one or more of the historic waterside pubs.

I provide a detailed route description for the 16 walks, together with maps, photographs and a brief historical introduction to each walk. Approximately 15 stops along each walk are selected for more detailed description and suggestions on what you should look out for. Guidance is given on visits to places of interest which have free entry. There are also full listings, including opening times and entrance fees, for all attractions on the route.

My aim is to inspire the reader to take a fresh look at the most magical parts of London by exploring its rivers, docks and canals on foot.

INTRODUCTION

London is here because of the River Thames. The Romans founded the city after their conquest of Britain in AD 43 on the site roughly between today's Blackfriars and the Tower of London. They chose this area because it was then the tidal limit of the Thames, and they could use the two daily tides to speed the transport of goods between London and the rest of the Roman Empire across the North Sea and the Channel. Another advantage was the presence of two Thames tributaries: the Fleet – which provided a defence to the west – and the Walbrook – which flowed through the centre of the Roman city and was used for industrial purposes, such as leather tanning.

The river was then much wider and shallower than today. It has gradually become narrower through the centuries because of repeated embankment work. Royal and aristocratic palaces and mansions were built with watergates fronting the river, and ships sailed up the Thames in ever-increasing numbers to unload their cargoes at Queenhithe, Billingsgate and numerous other quays.

Until 1750 there was only one bridge over the Thames in central London – the world famous London Bridge, with its houses and shops and the gates where the heads of executed persons were displayed on spikes. London Bridge was built in the thirteenth century and lasted an amazing 600 years. With its 19 arches it proved not only a barrier to shipping, but also slowed down the tidal flow so that on several occasions in winter the Thames froze for weeks on end.

Frost Fairs were set up with entertainment booths, and whole oxen were roasted on the ice. The last Frost Fair was in 1814, shortly before a new bridge was built with much wider arches.

As the population grew, the central London tributaries became polluted and were covered over for use as overflow sewers. In the nineteenth century Thomas Crapper popularised the water closet and as a result, so much sewage flowed into the Thames that cholera became rife, as this same water was recycled into drinking fountains and rich people's houses. Despite much protest, nothing was done until 1858. That summer, when Parliament was sitting, the MPs found the smell from the river so unbearable that it was known as the Year of the Great Stink. Finally, they commissioned Sir Joseph Bazalgette to build sewers to trap the effluent before it reached the Thames, and send it out to sewage processing plants to the east of London. The main sewers were incorporated into the Thames embankments and they are still used today.

The loss of surface water due to the embankments was counteracted in the nineteenth century by the construction of the Regent's Canal around London from Brentford to Limehouse, and more importantly by the development of the docks. This resulted in vast inland water basins to the east of the Tower of London which were crowded with ships from the far corners of the world.

Today there are no cargoes or liners. London no longer depends on the Thames for its commerce. The palaces and mansions are no more. Fortunately there is still much evidence of the past history of London's waterways if you know what to look for. The aim of this book is to point out this evidence, so as to allow the walker to compare what these waterways and the associated buildings looked like in the past with what can be seen today.

GUIDE TO MAPS

The maps are designed for use in conjunction with the directions in the text, providing a simple guide to the route of each walk. For the sake of clarity, the maps have more detail in places where I consider precise directions are required than in places where the route is straightforward, and therefore are not to scale.

I recommend you have a current London street map at hand, as the continuous construction work may cause the accessible routes to change from time to time.

CHAPTER 1

Central London River Walks

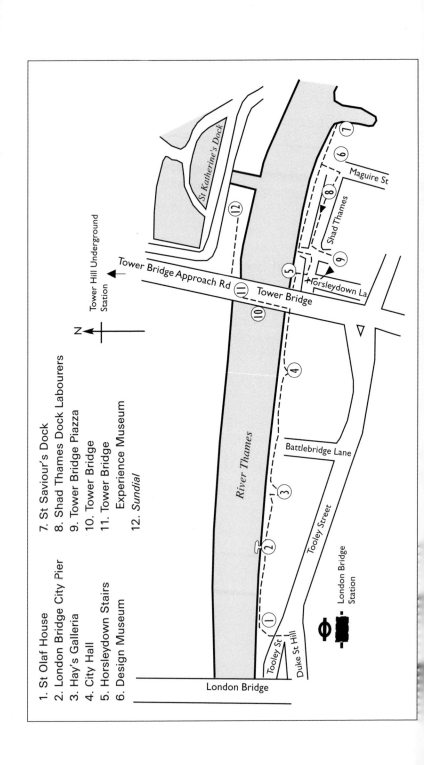

1. St Olaf House
2. London Bridge City Pier
3. Hay's Galleria
4. City Hall
5. Horsleydown Stairs
6. Design Museum
7. St Saviour's Dock
8. Shad Thames Dock Labourers
9. Tower Bridge Piazza
10. Tower Bridge
11. Tower Bridge Experience Museum
12. *Sundial*

St Katherine's Dock

Tower Hill Underground Station

Tower Bridge Approach Rd

N

Tower Bridge

Maguire St

Shad Thames

Horsleydown La

River Thames

Battlebridge Lane

Tooley Street

London Bridge Station

London Bridge

Tooley St

Duke St Hill

The Pool of London and Shad Thames

START: London Bridge Station (Tooley Street exit – this station has several exits, so if you are not familiar with it, ask station staff for directions). Cross Tooley Street via the pedestrian crossing, and walk straight on, bearing left past London Bridge Hospital towards the river.

FINISH: St Katherine's Dock – the nearest Underground is Tower Hill.

WALKING DISTANCE: 2 miles

HIGHLIGHTS: Hay's Galleria, City Hall, Tower Bridge, Butler's Wharf.

FOOD & DRINK: Hay's Galleria (snacks, cafés, Horniman at Hay's pub), Butler's Wharf area (full range of restaurants from Conran's flagship 'Pont de la Tour' to cheap cafés), St Katherine's Dock (The Dickens Inn, snack bars).

This walk takes you along the South Bank, which until 40 years ago was built up with wharves for handling all sorts of cargo. It was a hive of activity and not at all attractive for tourists or walkers. Today some wharves have been pulled down for modern developments, but many remain and have been converted for leisure use or as luxury apartments. Fortunately the conversions have been sensitively done and allow us to appreciate the industrial architecture and even some of the atmosphere of the old Port of London. The views are stunning.

1. ST OLAF HOUSE

The white building here is called St Olaf House, and on the south-west corner you can see an inlaid depiction of St Olaf.

St Olaf was born in AD 995 and was originally a Viking raider. He became King of Norway, after converting to Christianity in England and fighting with the Saxon King

Ethelred against the Danes. He is said to have tied ropes from his ships to the wooden posts of London Bridge and pulled it down to drown the Danish army as it crossed. This is the legend behind the famous nursery rhyme 'London Bridge is falling down'. He was later martyred when killed in battle in 1030 after Norway rejected his Christianity. Many miraculous circumstances occasioned around the time of his death, and as a result he was made a saint.

Until 1920 St Olave's Church was on this site. Lily Langtry, actress and mistress of Edward VII, spent her childhood here as her father was the curate. In 1930 the decline in church attendance resulted in the Hay's Wharf Company, who owned the wharves here, being granted approval to pull it down to build this prestigious modern office block in art deco style. The architects were Goodhart-Rendel. Note the doorway with black granite and glazed pottery surround. Above it are the coats of arms of three nineteenth-century Hay's Wharf families, in bright enamel on copper.

Walk on the left of St Olaf House to the river, then turn right along the Thames Path in the direction of Tower Bridge for about 100 metres. Stop by the pier in front of the Cottons Centre.

2. LONDON BRIDGE CITY PIER

There is a fine view of the City from here. You can identify some of the buildings across the river from the panoramic display near the pier. On the left, just this side of London Bridge, is Adelaide House, another art deco building from the 1930s. To the right of the modern blue-glass HSBC office block is Billingsgate, an attractive yellow-brick low-rise building. The architect was Horace Jones, who also designed Tower Bridge. This used to house London's fish market, but the market moved to Docklands in 1990. Today the building is mainly used for corporate functions. Next comes Custom House, another nineteenth-century building. This is at least the sixth Custom House on this site since the Customs Office was founded in the fourteenth century. The first Customs

Officer was Geoffrey Chaucer, who is far more famous for his *Canterbury Tales*, which started in The Tabard Inn not far from here, to the south of London Bridge.

The warship moored nearby is HMS *Belfast*. It was launched in 1938 and is the last surviving big-gun Second World War battleship. It led the 1944 Normandy bombardment for the D-Day landings. It last fought in the Korean War, and was decommissioned in 1965. It can now be visited as a museum, however its guns are still in working order and fired a salute at the 1995 V-E Day 50th anniversary celebrations. In 2002 it sailed under Tower Bridge to Southampton for refurbishment.

Continue along the river path to Hay's Galleria, which is a tall open space, covered by a glass canopy, lined with shops and cafés.

3. HAY'S GALLERIA

See the display at the entrance which shows the original dock built in 1856 by William Cubitt to enable tea clippers to unload tea from China. The dock also pioneered cold storage facilities and became known as 'London's Larder', as most imported perishable food was unloaded here. The whole stretch from London Bridge to Tower Bridge was owned by the Hay's Wharf Company. The original structure survived the 1980 redevelopment, but the dock was filled in and the glass canopy installed. It is fun trying to identify the seafaring themes on the large sculpture, *The Navigator*, in the centre of the Galleria. If you are lucky, waterworks will start up and set the Roman-style oars in motion.

Return to the river path out of the Galleria and proceed towards Tower Bridge until you come to the leaning glass building which looks a bit like a snail.

4. CITY HALL

City Hall was designed by Norman Foster for the Greater London Authority, London's strategic governing body. The

City Hall's modern glass-
and-steel structure
contrasting with the
Victorian Gothic
Tower Bridge

building is cooled by water from underground, and the
strange-looking tilt helps by angling just a small area of the
glass surface directly into the sun. Heat generated by the
computers and lights is recycled through the building's core.
As a result of these and many other environmental features,
City Hall uses only 25 per cent of the power of other similar-
sized buildings. There are several buildings by Norman
Foster in London, including the Swiss Re tower, the tall
glass structure shaped like a gherkin (as indeed most
Londoners know it) which you can see towering above most
of the City skyscrapers across the river.

Enter City Hall by the front doors. You will be searched
for security reasons before you go up to the second floor.
Here you can see the debating chamber and enjoy splendid
views of the river and the eleventh-century Tower of
London on the other side. Unfortunately the number of
bureaucrats has already outgrown this building and some
are having to work in less dramatic office spaces.

After leaving City Hall, carry on along the river path until you
come to the first building on your left after passing under
Tower Bridge.

5. HORSLEYDOWN STAIRS

By the entrance steps you will see a plaque describing the history of the building, which used to house the Anchor Brewery. You can walk up these steps for a magnificent view across the river. If the tide is out you can go down on to the pebbles of the riverbed and feel Tower Bridge looming above you. It is a thrilling experience. Be very careful, though, as the tide comes in fast. The name 'Horsleydown Stairs' comes from the seventeenth century, when horses used to bring hops and deliver beer here. When the horses needed a rest the drivers said 'Horse lie down'. Today the brewery and wharves have been converted into luxury apartments with stunning views. Look into the estate agent windows to see if you can afford to buy one.

Now walk along the cobbled road until you come to a narrow passage on the left called Maggie Blake's Cause, which takes you back to the river path. Continue along this path, noting the old anchors, propellers and other shipping tackle laid out like pieces of sculpture, until you come to a rectangular white building, set back 30 metres from the riverside.

6. DESIGN MUSEUM

This building houses the Design Museum. It was designed by Terence Conran of the Butler's Wharf Company, which redeveloped the area in the 1980s. Conran also set up the exclusive Pont de la Tour restaurant you will have just passed. The Design Museum has displays on twentieth-century mass-production design, from cutlery and chairs to electronic goods and cars. The chief executive as of 2003 is Charles Dyson, inventor of the bagless vacuum cleaner. Note the sculpture by Eduardo Paolozzi in front of the museum, which is well worth detailed examination. The same sculptor crafted the mosaics at Tottenham Court Road Underground Station.

Now walk as far as the bridge over the long water inlet you will find about 200 metres beyond the Design Museum.

7. ST SAVIOUR'S DOCK

The old warehouses on either side of this inlet have been converted into apartments. You will see their names, Butler's Wharf and New Concordia Wharf, inscribed on the top of the buildings. Note the pink façade of China Wharf just beyond New Concordia Wharf. John Cleese was dangled upside down from here in a classic scene from the film *A Fish Called Wanda*.

This inlet used to be the mouth of the River Neckinger, which rose by the Imperial War Museum and flowed under Elephant & Castle, New Kent Road and Abbey Street (the site of Bermondsey Abbey until the sixteenth century), before reaching St Saviour's Dock which was owned by the monks of Bermondsey Abbey. The name of the river comes from the 'Devil's neckinger' or noose, which was used to hang pirates caught here until the eighteenth century. The river was covered over in the nineteenth century except for its mouth. Across the bridge is the area known as Jacob's Island. Dickens describes it in *Oliver Twist* as 'the filthiest, strangest, most extraordinary of the many localities that are hidden in London', and this is where the novel's chief villain, Bill Sykes, meets his end.

Walk back along the path. Just past the Design Museum turn left inland, then immediately right into the cobbled road called Shad Thames. Continue onwards and soon on the right you see a plaque with a photograph of hundreds of dockers.

8. SHAD THAMES DOCK LABOURERS

The dockers in the photograph are shown waiting in the hope of being called for a day's work. Originally dockers had no permanent employment and were paid only when work was available. This system of casual labour was the cause of much industrial unrest. This ceased with the creation of the National Dock Labour Board in the 1940s, after which dockers were paid a retainer even if they did no work. In 1970 casual labour was abolished entirely and dockers were paid a fixed weekly wage. This cobbled road is reminiscent of the former Port of London, with the high-level walkways giving access from the riverside wharves to the distribution depots inland. Today it is lined with restaurants and bars.

Walk to the end of the cobbled road and turn left into Tower Bridge Piazza.

9. TOWER BRIDGE PIAZZA

This square houses a fountain designed by Antony Donaldson in 1991, incorporating female forms around a metal tub. Many objects have been left beside it which on closer inspection are pieces of sculpture. The watch is particularly realistic.

Now walk back under Tower Bridge and ascend the stairs on the west side of the bridge. Walk to the centre of the bridge where you will find a display identifying the buildings upstream, many of which you have already seen.

10. TOWER BRIDGE

Tower Bridge was designed by architect Horace Jones and was opened in 1894 by the Prince of Wales. The design

Tower Bridge's bascules are still frequently raised, but no longer by hydraulic power

for the bridge had to include a drawbridge to allow the many tall cargo ships access to the wharves in the Pool of London, the area between here and London Bridge. On one occasion in the 1950s a bus driver was crossing the bridge when the drawbridge started to rise. He made a quick decision to accelerate and managed to jump the opening gap just in time.

The two 1,000-ton bascules can be raised in 90 seconds. They were operated by hydraulic power until the 1970s, but today use electricity. Even now they are raised quite often and it is a fantastic sight if you are lucky enough to be there when a ship passes through.

Carry on over the bridge until you come to the entrance to the Tower Bridge Experience, for which there is an admission charge.

11. TOWER BRIDGE EXPERIENCE MUSEUM

Inside you can see the beautiful hydraulic machinery which used to operate the drawbridge, and you can also go up to the top walkway, which provides unique views upstream and downstream. The walkway was constructed because the drawbridge was in frequent use at the time and it provided an alternative passage for pedestrians. It stands 60 feet above the road and 135 feet above the Thames at high tide. Most people preferred to wait for the drawbridge to be lowered rather than climb to the top, so the walkway was closed in 1910. Just past the museum is the north-west tower of the bridge, on which is a plaque commemorating the 1994 centenary of its opening.

Walk on past the tower and go down the stairs on your left. You emerge on the other side of the bridge in front of the forbidding concrete block of the Tower Thistle Hotel, which was the first part of the former St Katherine's Dock to be redeveloped in the 1970s. At the bottom of the stairs note the sign reading 'Dead man's hole' in front of the small pebbled beach under the bridge. This, it is claimed, is where bodies dumped in the river used to be found. From here you have a good view of City Hall across the river. Carry on along the riverbank until you come to the *Sundial* sculpture.

12. *SUNDIAL*

The *Sundial* sculpture by Wendy Taylor, and the *Girl with a Dolphin* by David Wynne that you have just passed, were erected in 1973. They both seem appropriate for this area, which was so connected with seafaring in the past. There are also fine views of Tower Bridge, and across the river to the Anchor Brewery and Butler's Wharf developments you have just left. St Katherine's Dock, which is described in the Wapping and the London Docks walk in Chapter 3, is just ahead.

The walk ends here. There are several eating establishments in St Katherine's Dock. For the nearest Underground station, walk back to Tower Bridge, ascend the stairs and walk along Tower Bridge Approach Road to Tower Hill Underground Station (District and Circle Line). Alternatively, if you want to go back to London Bridge Station, cross over Tower Bridge – this is less than a 20-minute walk.

Grand Turk, a replica eighteenth-century warship,
sailing out of St Katherine's Dock

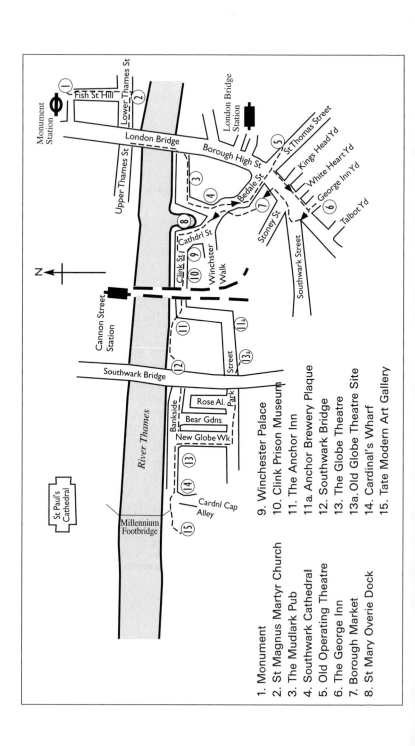

1. Monument
2. St Magnus Martyr Church
3. The Mudlark Pub
4. Southwark Cathedral
5. Old Operating Theatre
6. The George Inn
7. Borough Market
8. St Mary Overie Dock
9. Winchester Palace
10. Clink Prison Museum
11. The Anchor Inn
11a. Anchor Brewery Plaque
12. Southwark Bridge
13. The Globe Theatre
13a. Old Globe Theatre Site
14. Cardinal's Wharf
15. Tate Modern Art Gallery

Southwark

START: Monument Underground Station (Monument exit).
FINISH: Tate Modern Art Gallery – the nearest Underground is Blackfriars or Southwark.
WALKING DISTANCE: 1¾ miles
HIGHLIGHTS: Monument, St Magnus Martyr Church, London Bridge, Southwark Cathedral, The George Inn, the *Golden Hind*, Clink Prison Museum, The Globe Theatre, Tate Modern Art Gallery.
FOOD & DRINK: The Mudlark pub, The George Inn, The Anchor Inn, The Globe Theatre restaurant, The Founder's Arms.

This walk begins at Sir Christopher Wren's Monument to the Great Fire of London of 1666. Across London Bridge on the South Bank of the Thames is the district of Southwark, which has always been outside the control of the City of London. The name probably comes from 'South Work'. It used to have a murky reputation and often provided the entertainment, work and trade that city dwellers wanted but were not permitted within the boundaries of the city. Here you will visit sites connected with Shakespeare, Chaucer and the Bishops of Winchester, as well as ancient inns, hospitals, markets and prisons. The walk ends at the massive former Bankside Power Station, now converted into one of London's top tourist attractions – the Tate Modern Art Gallery.

1. MONUMENT
Look up to the top of this tall obelisk, which was designed by Sir Christopher Wren to commemorate the Great Fire of London of 1666. You will see a golden urn which gives out a fiery glow in the sunshine. The urn is at a height of 202 feet, which is the exact distance to the baker's shop in

Pudding Lane where the fire started. Pudding Lane still exists to the east of the Monument and there is a plaque on the building at its corner with Monument Street describing how the fire started in the nearby baker's shop.

Within three days, 80 per cent of the old city was burnt down, including 87 churches and Old St Paul's Cathedral. Amazingly, only six people were killed. One was the unfortunate Agent Hubert, who fell foul of the anti-Catholic feelings of the time. He was falsely accused of starting the fire and then executed. You can see a Latin inscription on the north side of the Monument with the bottom line missing. This used to have words blaming the Catholics and was only removed after the Catholic Emancipation Act of 1829.

The fire had spread rapidly partly because most of the houses in the city were built of wood and plaster. Very few of these structures remain, as all new buildings after 1666 had to be constructed from brick and stone, thus completely changing the character of London. After the fire, Sir Christopher Wren was made responsible for rebuilding 51 of the old Norman and Gothic churches, mainly in the baroque style. He also produced a grand plan to reconstruct the whole city with a grid of wide boulevards to rival Paris. This was thought to be too ambitious however, so we are left with much the same street pattern as in the Middle Ages.

Walk down Fish Street Hill to Lower Thames Street, and cross this by the pedestrian traffic lights. Now enter the small churchyard of St Magnus Martyr to the west end of the church.

2. ST MAGNUS MARTYR CHURCH

Sir Christopher Wren built this church in 1676, but the splendid tower and clock were added in the 1700s. The church is well worth a visit as it contains much original seventeenth-century wood carving and wrought ironwork. Inside you will also see a model of the thirteenth-century London Bridge with its houses and

Chapel of St Thomas in the middle. This was considered one of the greatest tourist attractions in the land and lasted over 600 years. The approach to the bridge went through this churchyard, and you can see some of its stones opposite the church entrance. In 1831 a new London Bridge was constructed by John Rennie about 100 metres to the west of the original bridge. This was sold to an American for £1 million in 1970 and can now be seen at Lake Havasu in Arizona. Although it makes a good story, there is no truth in the rumour that the American thought he was buying Tower Bridge. The London Bridge we see today is on the same site as Rennie's bridge, but was built much wider to cater for the large number of commuters who cross it to and from work in the City.

Turn left out of the churchyard and walk the short distance to London Bridge. As soon as you reach the bridge, turn left up the steps to a walkway halfway up the bridge. Do not go up the final flight of steps on this (eastern) side, but walk under the bridge to emerge up the steps on the far (western) side. Now cross the bridge until you reach the south side of the river. Here go down the steep steps on your right to Montague Close and then turn right.

3. THE MUDLARK PUB

Here you will see The Mudlark pub sign. Mudlarks were poor children, as shown on this sign, or old people who scavenged the riverbanks at low tide. They earned about a halfpenny a day, mainly from lumps of coal dropped from barges. Their abject poverty is described in the novels of Charles Dickens.

Another Dickens connection is the steps you have just descended. These are called 'Nancy's Steps' as this is where, in *Oliver Twist*, Nancy has her ill-fated conversation with Mr Brownlow when she tells him that Oliver is in the hands of Bill Sykes. She is overheard and this leads to her brutal murder. The arch over the road which goes under the bridge by Nancy's Steps is one of the few remains from John Rennie's London Bridge, which was the bridge Dickens knew.

Now carry on past Southwark Cathedral, and walk to the left until you reach the gates to the Cathedral's south entrance.

4. SOUTHWARK CATHEDRAL

There has been a church on this site ever since Saxon times, but the earliest remains are from the 1106 Norman church, built by monks of the Augustinian order. In 1212 this was largely destroyed by fire, and a new church, predating Westminster Abbey, was built in the Early English Gothic style. It became a cathedral in 1905 when the new Diocese of Southwark was created.

Inside you will see beautiful architecture from the earliest Norman remains to the fine nineteenth-century restoration of the nave. There are also many splendid monuments, including a twentieth-century stained-glass window commemorating William Shakespeare and his most famous plays, and a chapel dedicated to John Harvard, founder of Harvard University, who was born in Southwark. A donation of £2.50 is requested to enter the cathedral.

Go on southwards down Cathedral Street and its continuation, Bedale Street, until you reach Borough High Street. Cross by the pedestrian crossing and walk about 30 metres up St Thomas Street, where you will see a Georgian red-brick church tower on the left.

5. OLD OPERATING THEATRE

Within the roof space of this church is the oldest operating theatre in Britain. This is all that remains of the old St Thomas's Hospital, which was founded in the twelfth century by the Augustinian monks who also built the Norman church.

Today it is a museum where you can see an exhibition of medieval herbal remedies as well as the theatre itself, where students could watch the surgeon at work. The operating

The Church of St Thomas, built in 1703, houses the Old Operating Theatre in its roof space

table has a box of sawdust underneath. This was used to soak up blood from the patients, who underwent surgery without the benefit of anaesthetics. St Thomas's Hospital itself was moved to Lambeth in the nineteenth century.

Turn right and proceed down Borough High Street until you come to George Inn Yard.

6. THE GEORGE INN

Many inns were located here for travellers coming in and out of London, as the gates of London Bridge were closed at night. The most famous one was The Tabard Inn where Chaucer's *Canterbury Tales* began. Southwark was always renowned for the excellent variety of its beer. Chaucer has the Miller say at the start of his tale:

> If the words get muddled in my tale,
> Just put it down to too much Southwark ale.

He then proceeds to tell the most obscene of all the tales, despite the efforts of mine host to stop him. The Tabard

Inn no longer exists, but used to be in Talbot Yard just to the south.

The George Inn is the only remaining galleried inn in London. It was built in 1676 on the site of a previous inn which had been destroyed by fire. As well as providing refreshment and accommodation for travellers, the inn was also used by travelling actors to perform plays in the courtyard. Originally there were galleries on all four sides, but today only two sides are left. Elizabethan theatres like The Globe were probably modelled on this type of inn.

Now cross back over Borough High Street and Southwark Street by the pedestrian crossing. Turn right and after 50 metres enter left under the glass canopy of Borough Market.

7. BOROUGH MARKET

Here you will find stalls for the sale of a wide variety of high-quality fruit and vegetables. The market is currently open to the public on Friday afternoons and 9 a.m.–4 p.m. on Saturdays. It is the oldest such market in central London and traces its origins to 1014, when it was situated by London Bridge. In 1756 it was moved to its present site to ease the traffic flow over the bridge. It is said that the pillories set up here were especially popular due to the ready supply of rotten tomatoes. It is to be hoped that plans to improve the rail links that run over the top of the market will not endanger its survival.

Walk through the market, exit back into Cathedral Street, and carry on past the Cathedral towards the river to Clink Street.

8. ST MARY OVERIE DOCK

This dock is named after the original Saxon church built here 'over the river'. This term is used to indicate the South Bank of the Thames, which is on the opposite side of the river from the City of London. It was one of the many docks and wharves where ships landed their cargoes until the Port of London closed down in the 1960s.

Today, the *Golden Hind* is moored here – a replica of the ship in which Sir Francis Drake circumnavigated the world before being knighted by Queen Elizabeth I. It was built in 1973, based on research into what Elizabethan warships looked like and has itself sailed all over the world.

Walk along Clink Street until you come to a Gothic ruin on your left.

9. WINCHESTER PALACE

The ruins of the fourteenth-century Great Hall of the London Palace of the Bishops of Winchester are an unexpected sight in this narrow street, lined with converted warehouses. The architect of the Great Hall, with its fine rose window, was Henry Yevele, who also designed much of Canterbury Cathedral.

The Bishops of Winchester were among the most powerful people in England in medieval times. As Winchester itself was remote from the monarch's Palace of Westminster, they needed to establish a London residence. Bishop William Giffard built the original palace here in 1109 and soon the whole area of Southwark came under the control of the Bishops of Winchester until Cromwell destroyed their influence in the seventeenth century. After that the palace was turned to various other uses including that of a mustard factory. The palace ruins were rediscovered following a fire in the nineteenth century. A plaque describes its history.

Continue about 100 metres along Clink Street where you will find Clink Prison Museum on the left.

10. CLINK PRISON MUSEUM

This museum shows graphic details of the punishments and torture practised in the old Clink prison. It was under the jurisdiction of the Bishops of Winchester and many dissenters were imprisoned here. In Elizabethan times, the many theatres in the area provided a plentiful supply of inmates for the prison as actors were often involved in brawls and even murder. The name comes from the Saxon word 'clench', meaning 'chain', and is still used in the colloquial expression 'in the clink'.

Walk to the end of Clink Street.

11. THE ANCHOR INN

Ahead is The Anchor Inn with its river terrace outside, and dining rooms and bars dating from the eighteenth century inside. An earlier inn on this site was near enough to The Globe Theatre for Shakespeare and his fellow actors to have used it for their changing rooms and drinking bouts. The present inn was built in 1775 and owned by Mr and Mrs Thrale, who were friends of Dr Johnson. Upstairs are hideaways where fugitives from the Clink prison could find refuge. Just round the corner in Park Street is a plaque denoting where the Thrales also owned a brewery. The beer was brewed from Thames water and the pollution no doubt added to the taste. To your left is Vinopolis which also serves food, but is better known for its wine-tasting.

Carry on along the Thames Path in front of The Anchor to Southwark Bridge.

12. SOUTHWARK BRIDGE

Southwark Bridge was built in 1920, replacing an earlier cast-iron bridge of 1819 by John Rennie. The modern office block on the east side of the bridge is home to the *Financial Times*. Across the river you can see the monumental towers of Cannon Street Mainline Station. They survived bombing during the Second World War, but the segmental arched-iron train shed was badly damaged. It was eventually replaced in 1987 by the white 'air rights' block which projects like a ship's prow between the towers.

Under Southwark Bridge you can see slate murals showing scenes from the Frost Fairs which used to take place when the Thames froze over for weeks on end. The last fair was in 1814. Shortly after that the Old London Bridge with its 19 arches was pulled down and the improved flow of the river meant that it no longer froze over in winter.

Pass under the bridge and along the Thames Path until you reach The Globe.

13. THE GLOBE THEATRE

The Globe was opened in 1997, the brainchild of American actor, Sam Wannamaker, who died shortly before its completion. It was built as much as possible from the same materials as the original Globe Theatre – unseasoned oak, lime plaster and thatch. The differences include the water sprinklers that are just visible in the roof and the presence of toilets. Elizabethan audiences stood on sawdust in front of the stage and did not bother with such modern conveniences. They also tended to take part in the action, booing or cheering depending on whether they liked the actors. Even today the atmosphere in The Globe is very different from the respectful appreciation shown in West End theatres, as audience participation is encouraged.

The first permanent theatre in London, built in Shoreditch in 1576, was simply called 'The Theatre'. The Burbage brothers owned the company which performed there, and Shakespeare also had a share in it. When the lease ran out in 1598, the company moved it to a site in Park Street just the other side of Southwark Bridge. There is a plaque in front of the block of flats that has been built on top of it. You might like to make the detour to visit the site where you will also see the famous seventeenth-century panorama of Southwark by Wenceslaus Hollar, showing the several theatres which sprang up here around

The Globe Theatre, reconstructed using traditional materials, but with water sprinklers just visible on the thatched roof

that time. These were The Hope, The Rose and The Swan as well as The Globe. They were used for bull- and bear-baiting as well as for plays. Samuel Pepys records with excitement how a dog was tossed right into his box by a bull.

All of Shakespeare's great tragedies and history plays were performed here until 1613, when a canon fired during a performance of *Henry VIII* caused a fire and the theatre burned down. Nobody was killed, but it was recorded that one man's breeches caught fire, although he managed to put out the fire by pouring a bottle of ale over himself.

Plays are performed throughout the summer regardless of the weather. You can also have a guided tour of the theatre and enjoy a meal with an impressive view of the river from the restaurant on the corner of New Globe Walk.

Carry on past The Globe until you see a row of houses at Cardinal Cap Alley.

14. CARDINAL'S WHARF

Note the house with the sign of a cardinal's hat. This dates from the sixteenth century, although the front was plastered over later. Prostitution was rife here on Bankside until Oliver Cromwell put a stop to it in the middle of the seventeenth century. Brothels stood all along the riverbank, each with their own signs. Many were owned by the Bishops of Winchester as is evident from the cardinal's hat. The prostitutes wore cream dresses and waved to potential customers across the river in the City. They therefore became known as 'Winchester Geese'. Ferrymen waited at the many stairs on the riverbanks to take the men across, with loud cries of 'Oars! Oars!', much to the amusement of the expectant whores on the other side. Next door is the Provost's lodging, dating from 1710.

Now continue along the Thames Path to the Tate Modern Art Gallery.

15. TATE MODERN ART GALLERY

The Tate Modern Art Gallery was opened in this former power station in 2001. It is now one of London's most popular visitor attractions and entry is free.

The original oil-fired power station was designed by the architect Sir Giles Gilbert Scott, who was also responsible for Battersea Power Station and Waterloo Bridge. It opened in 1963, but had to close down in 1981 due to the rise in oil prices. It lay derelict until chosen as the ideal space for expanding the Tate Gallery's modern (post-nineteenth century) international collection. The conversion was carried out by the Swiss team of Herzog and de Meuron. The architects have managed to preserve the integrity of Scott's original design, while adding the large glass structure which spans the length of the roof in order to let natural light into the top-floor galleries.

Enter by the riverside entrance into the vast space of the former turbine hall where there is a changing exhibition or large sculpture display. Then ascend to the

The Millennium Footbridge
leading from the Tate
Modern Art Gallery to St
Paul's Cathedral

fifth floor galleries to find a viewing area overlooking the Thames. From here there is a stunning view of St Paul's Cathedral which can be accessed via the Millennium Footbridge outside the gallery. This bridge was opened in 2001 to a great fanfare, but the crowds who crossed it caused it to wobble so much that it had to be closed for a year until it was stabilised. It is still known to Londoners as the 'Wobbly Bridge' even though, to the disappointment of many of us, the wobble has now vanished.

The walk ends here. It is now possible to walk over the footbridge to St Paul's Cathedral, as mentioned before, or alternatively, carry on along the Thames Path to Blackfriars Bridge, and cross over the bridge to Blackfriars Underground and Mainline Station. If you walk the other way, down Blackfriars Road, it will lead you to Southwark Underground Station.

Blackfriars, Temple and Embankment

START: Blackfriars Underground Station (exit 1 by The Black Friar pub).
FINISH: Embankment Underground Station.
WALKING DISTANCE: 1½ miles
HIGHLIGHTS: Blackfriars Bridge, Temple Church, Middle Temple Hall, Somerset House, Cleopatra's Needle, York Watergate.
FOOD & DRINK: The Black Friar, The Devereux and The Edgar Wallace pubs, Somerset House café and restaurant, The Savoy Hotel, Gordon's Wine Bar.

The art nouveau Black Friar pub recalls the great Dominican monastery situated here until the dissolution of the monasteries in 1536. The River Fleet flowed into the Thames at Blackfriars until the eighteenth century. Today you can descend to the Thames Path and see the strange-looking ghost bridge (only the cast-iron piers remain) between the road and rail bridges of Blackfriars. Upstream is where the lawyers have resided since medieval times in the Inner and Middle Temple Inns of Court. In these courtyards, which are reminiscent of Oxford University colleges, are located the Norman Temple Church and the Elizabethan Middle Temple Hall as well as barristers' chambers dating from the eighteenth century. Next you come to Somerset House, an imposing building in the classical style, which houses two of London's finest art collections – the Courtauld Gallery and the Gilbert Collection. Finally, you pass the Savoy, one of London's most famous hotels, and see London's oldest monument, Cleopatra's Needle, before ending up at York Watergate where you discover how far the Thames stretched before the nineteenth-century embankments were built.

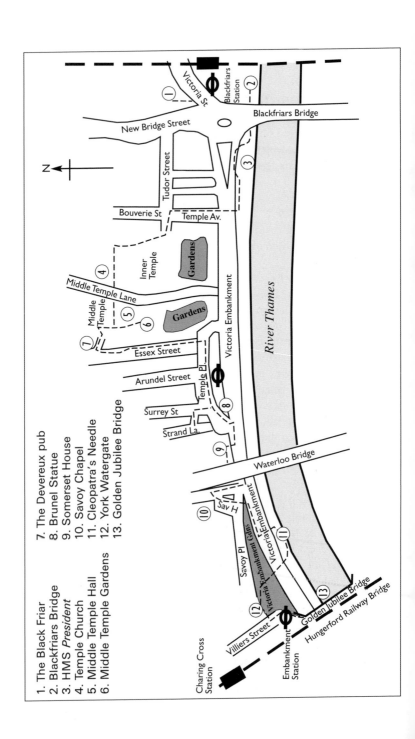

N

Victoria St

Blackfriars Station

Blackfriars Bridge

New Bridge Street

Tudor Street

Bouverie St

Temple Av.

Inner Temple

Gardens

Middle Temple Lane

Middle Temple

Gardens

Essex Street

Arundel Street

Temple Pl

Victoria Embankment

River Thames

Surrey St

Strand La.

Waterloo Bridge

Sav H

Savoy Pl

Savoy Embankment Gdns

Victoria Embankment

Charing Cross Station

Villiers Street

Embankment Station

Golden Jubilee Bridge

Hungerford Railway Bridge

1. The Black Friar
2. Blackfriars Bridge
3. HMS *President*
4. Temple Church
5. Middle Temple Hall
6. Middle Temple Gardens
7. The Devereux pub
8. Brunel Statue
9. Somerset House
10. Savoy Chapel
11. Cleopatra's Needle
12. York Watergate
13. Golden Jubilee Bridge

1. THE BLACK FRIAR

This is the site of Blackfriars Monastery, founded in the thirteenth century by the Dominicans. Henry VIII entertained the Holy Roman Emperor Charles V here on his visit in 1525, but he dissolved the monastery shortly afterwards in 1538 and nothing remains except a piece of its wall in New Ireland Yard, a short walk past the back of the pub. The pub itself was built in 1900 in the art nouveau style. The statue of a portly friar implies that good food and drink are still available here, thus keeping up the hospitable reputation of the former monastery. You can see a mosaic above the pub entrance, showing two friars catching a plump salmon in the river flowing past their monastery. This was the River Fleet, which flowed along what is now New Bridge Street.

Looking towards the Thames you can see the impressive curved classical façade of Unilever House, built in the 1930s as the most prestigious Head Office at the time. In the middle of the road at the approach to Blackfriars Bridge is a statue of Queen Victoria. She opened the bridge in 1869 at the same time as Holborn Viaduct, which you can see to the north, crossing over Farringdon Road, which is the continuation of New

The art nouveau Black Friar, standing on the site of the former Blackfriars Monastery

41

Bridge Street. At the time she was very unpopular with the public and the crowd hissed at her – she had been a long time in mourning for Prince Albert and had kept herself from the public eye. As shown in the film, *Mrs Brown*, it was her Scottish servant, Mr Brown, who finally persuaded her to resume her public duties and by the time of her Diamond Jubilee in 1897 a million-strong crowd cheered her procession up Fleet Street to St Paul's Cathedral.

Go down the steps to the underpass and keep on to exit 6. Now go down to the Thames Path and walk downstream until you come to the open air and a pleasant seating area.

2. BLACKFRIARS BRIDGE

Here you can admire the road bridge, with its five wrought iron arches on granite piers. The abutments supporting the bridge have carved semicircular projecting balustrades on top, resembling pulpits. This was done at the request of Queen Victoria to remind people of the former monastery. It was built by Joseph Cubitt. In 1982 the Italian banker, Roberto Calvi, was found hanging at Blackfriars Bridge. Mafia involvement was suspected, but at the time of writing there have been no arrests. An earlier bridge was built here in 1769 when the River Fleet was finally covered over because it had become polluted. Today the Fleet is used as an overflow sewer. If you look over the river wall, you can see a ladder descending to the riverbed. At the bottom, when the tide is out, you can see an arch in the river wall where the culverted River Fleet flows into the Thames.

Just downstream are the remaining cast iron columns of the first Blackfriars Railway Bridge built in 1864, also by Joseph Cubitt. The bridge itself was removed in 1985 as the later railway bridge you can see to the east started taking trains over the river to a new Blackfriars Station. Inside this station, by Platform 4, you can see stone blocks from the original station of the former London, Dover and Chatham Railway inscribed with its many destinations, including such unlikely companions as Bromley and Vienna. Under the bridge you have a view of the former Bankside Power Station now housing the Tate Modern Art Gallery.

Now walk back under the road bridge and ascend the steps up to the west side of the bridge. Continue westwards along the Embankment until you come to the moored ship, HMS *President* by the pedestrian crossing opposite Temple Lane.

3. HMS *PRESIDENT*

This is one of many historic ships now moored by the Thames in central London. It was a 1918 warship, now converted into the headquarters of Interaction, a charity set up in 1968 to help inner-city families. Look across the river where you see the tall building with the mosaic letters OXO inscribed on the front. This was a ploy to advertise OXO cubes in the 1930s when the tower was built and advertising was forbidden on the banks of the Thames. Today it is part of the Coin Street development, which provides low-cost housing for local people as well as craft studios and, on the top, an exclusive Harvey Nichols restaurant.

Looking back towards Blackfriars, you can see two distinctive nineteenth-century buildings. The grey Portland stone one next to Unilever is the former City of London School for Boys, built in 1882. The statues above the first-floor windows represent Britain's intellectual and literary giants. From left to right they are Milton, Bacon, Newton and Shakespeare. The school has since moved to a site on the river below St Paul's and J.P. Morgan now occupies this building. Next is Sion College, an 1887 red-brick Victorian Gothic building by Sir Arthur Blomfield. The theological college was dissolved in 1996 and the building is now used as offices.

Further along the bank, cross the main road and go up Temple Avenue to Tudor Street. Turn left and walk to the end to the gates of Inner Temple. Enter the gates and walk to the right across the courtyard known as King's Bench Walk. In the north-west corner of the courtyard there is a path between Inner Temple Library and Francis Taylor Buildings. Go through into Church Court.

4. TEMPLE CHURCH

The Knights Templar built the Great House of the New Temple and Temple Church here in 1185. The west part is the original round church in the Norman style, modelled on the Church of the Holy Sepulchre in Jerusalem. In the thirteenth century, the longer east part was built in the Gothic style. It is well worth a visit to see the beautiful mixture of Norman and Gothic architecture and fine monuments, including the almost uncanny effigies of thirteenth-century knights lying on the floor of the round church.

Today this serves as the church of both the Inner and Middle Temple, which are two of the four Inns of Court – the others being Lincoln's Inn and Gray's Inn. All barristers belong to at least one of these inns. Now is not the time to go into the fascinating history of the Inns of Court. Suffice it to say that when the Templars were disbanded in the fourteenth century, lawyers set up in this area as it was strategically placed by the river between the trading centre of the City of London and the Royal Palace at Westminster. Originally they had lodgings here, hence the name 'Inn'. Today the barristers work in 'Chambers', but very few actually have apartments here.

The statue on a column in the middle of Church Court was erected in 2002. This shows two knights on a horse and is the origin of the Inner Temple sign of Pegasus, the flying horse of Greek mythology. The Pegasus image can be seen in many places in Inner Temple, including the top of the drainpipes of Inner Temple Hall opposite the church.

After visiting the church, walk under the cloisters and through Pump Court to the west till you come to Middle Temple Lane. Turn left and then right up the steps into Fountain Court.

5. MIDDLE TEMPLE HALL

You have now entered Middle Temple, whose sign is the Lamb and Flag. The Hall dates from 1573 in the reign of Queen Elizabeth I. Do not be put off by the sign saying 'not open to the public' as it is usually open weekdays 10 a.m.–11.30 a.m. and 3 p.m.–4 p.m. Just ask the porter.

This is one of the most impressive Elizabethan Great Halls in England, with its double hammerbeam roof and oak screen. It is known that Queen Elizabeth herself often dined here, and she donated an oak tree from Windsor Park that was floated down the Thames to make the High Table. Note the portraits of several monarchs, the coats of arms of senior lawyers from the sixteenth century onwards, and the display of Elizabethan armour. It is recorded that Shakespeare took part in the first performance of *Twelfth Night* in front of the Queen in this hall.

Walk to the fountain at the end of the courtyard.

6. MIDDLE TEMPLE GARDENS

Look towards the Thames and you will see the rose garden where one of the most famous events in British history is supposed to have started – the Wars of the Roses. According to Shakespeare in *Henry VI Part I*, it was here that the Yorkists plucked a white rose and the Lancastrians a red rose. The wars finally ended when Richard III was defeated at the Battle of Bosworth Field in 1485. Then Henry VII started the Tudor dynasty, whose sign was the red and white combined Tudor rose you can see on the railings by Middle Temple Hall.

The fountain, with the ancient mulberry tree, is mentioned in Dickens's novel *Martin Chuzzlewit*. Here Ruth Pinch has an assignment with her lover.

Walk to the north-west corner of the courtyard, where a gateway leads you out of the Temple.

7. THE DEVEREUX PUB

This was a coffeehouse in the eighteenth century, but converted into a pub in 1843. Robert Devereux was the Earl of Essex and a favourite of Queen Elizabeth. He had a mansion here in Elizabethan times, stretching right down to the Thames. After a disastrous campaign in Ireland, Devereux rebelled against the Queen and was executed in the Tower of London. The mansion, like many others along the banks of the Thames, was pulled down in the seventeenth century and redeveloped to house the growing number of people who wanted to move away from the trading centre of the City. Next door is The Edgar Wallace pub, named after the author who was also a journalist working just up the road in Fleet Street.

Walk on to Essex Street, where you turn left. At the bottom of the street descend the steps and carry on to Temple Place. Turn right here and carry on past the Howard Hotel until you come to the Victoria Embankment.

8. BRUNEL STATUE

On the site of the Howard Hotel was the Tudor mansion of Thomas Howard, Earl of Arundel. Like most of the mansions on the North Bank, this was pulled down for redevelopment in the seventeenth century. You could take a short detour up Surrey Street opposite to see the only remaining part of the mansion – the so-called Roman Baths. You will find them down a small passageway on the left, which is signposted by the National Trust. The baths are still filled with water from one of the many underground springs that are to be found near the Thames in London.

The statue of Isambard Kingdom Brunel honours the famous Victorian engineer who undertook projects astonishing for their versatility and daring. With his father, Marc Brunel, he constructed under the Thames the world's first significant underwater tunnel. He also built railways, bridges and the world's largest iron steamship,

River god bust over the watergate at Somerset House

the *Great Eastern*. He was voted Britain's second greatest man after Winston Churchill in 2002.

Now carry on and turn right along the Embankment for about 100 metres when you will come to the arched entrance to Somerset House on your right.

9. SOMERSET HOUSE

Sir William Chambers designed this massive building in the 1770s in the classical style. It was finally completed when the east and west wings were added early in the next century, following Chambers's design. Standing at the arched entrance on the Embankment, you see what was the watergate at that time. The Thames then came right up to the heavily rusticated lower walls, and the Naval Office used this watergate for their ceremonial barge. Go into the building and descend the steps in the shop area to your left to see the splendidly decorated barge, which now lies on pebbles at the level of the Thames.

If you walk past the barge and up the stairs at the far end, you come to the café area further inside the building. Here you can see an excellent pictorial video presentation about the history of Somerset House, from its origins as the first Renaissance palace in England, built in 1550 for the Lord Protector Somerset, to its eighteenth-century reconstruction as government offices and home to the Royal Academy. The presentation runs continuously throughout the day and lasts about ten minutes. If you have time, go up in the lift to the right of the café and see the Seaman's Waiting Room with its portraits of admirals, including Lord Nelson. This is where the naval captains waited to be told of their next commissions. Go out of the north door into the courtyard, which has an ice-skating rink in winter and fountains during the rest of the year. Return and walk to the end of the corridor to the west to see the amazingly cantilevered Naval Staircase. Finally, go out of the south door to admire the front of the building from the river terrace.

Walk to the end of the terrace and descend the steps to go under Waterloo Bridge and emerge on the other side at the level of the Embankment. Walk up Savoy Hill past the statue of Michael Faraday, regarded as one of history's greatest experimental physicists, until you see a churchyard and Gothic chapel to your left.

10. SAVOY CHAPEL

In the thirteenth century the land here was granted to the Count of Savoie, who built a palace which was vastly extended by its later owners, the Dukes of Lancaster. The palace was virtually destroyed in the Peasants' Revolt of 1381. Henry VII had it rebuilt in 1505 as a hospital for the poor, and this chapel is the only remaining building. Today it is the Chapel of the Royal Victorian Order.

The rest of the hospital was finally pulled down to build the first Waterloo Bridge in 1817 and, later in the nineteenth century, the Savoy Theatre and Hotel, named after the ancient palace. The original Waterloo Bridge was replaced by today's cantilevered reinforced-concrete structure, faced in Portland stone. It was designed in 1942 by Sir Giles Gilbert Scott – also architect of Bankside Power Station which now houses the Tate Modern Art Gallery.

Walk past the front of the Chapel and then turn left down the extension of Savoy Hill back to the Embankment. Cross over to the riverside by the pedestrian crossing and walk to the right to the tall Egyptian obelisk.

11. CLEOPATRA'S NEEDLE

This 26-metre-high obelisk is London's oldest monument and was originally erected at Heliopolis. Cleopatra's Needle was a gift to Britain from the Turkish viceroy of Egypt, and only just survived a stormy sea voyage before being erected here in 1878. Its name is misleading as it dates from 1475 BC when the Pharaoh Tuthmosis III ruled Egypt. Cleopatra was the name of the boat which transported it to London. Several contemporary articles were buried underneath for posterity, including daily newspapers, a set of Victorian coins and photographs of 12 beautiful English women. The two sphinxes are nineteenth-century sculptures and strictly speaking should have been erected facing outwards. If you look carefully you will see shrapnel holes in them. These are from a First World War Zeppelin bomb. The cast-iron lampposts with carved dolphins that you can see all along the Embankment are

Cleopatra's Needle with one of the Victorian 'dolphin' lampposts which line the Embankment

49

also from the reign of Queen Victoria and most have a date stamped on them.

Cross back to the other side of the Embankment and go into the Victoria Embankment Gardens. Walk to the north-west corner past the bandstand to York Watergate.

12. YORK WATERGATE

This stone construction of three bays with rusticated bands on the columns used to be the watergate of York House, one of the aristocratic mansions with gardens stretching down to the Thames. The mansion is named after the Archbishop of York, who received it from Queen Mary in 1556. As with Somerset House, the owners favoured the use of the river for transport to and from the City and Westminster, to avoid the dirty and sometimes dangerously crowded roads.

The watergate you see here was built in 1626 for George Villiers, the Duke of Buckingham, who owned the mansion at the time. He was the favourite of James I and Charles I, who showered him with honours. He soon became one of the wealthiest and most powerful men in the land, but was murdered by a discontented subaltern as he was about to lead an expedition to France in 1627. In the 1670s his heirs decided to sell the mansion off to the speculative builder, Nicholas Barbon, to develop it into town houses. A condition of the sale was that the streets should be named after him. So there is a George Street, Villiers Street, Duke Street, Of Alley and Buckingham Street. The Council has unfortunately changed the name Of Alley to York Place, although the small lane at the top of Villiers Street still has the sign 'Formerly Of Alley'.

As you can see from the engraving near the watergate, the river used to come right up here. The engraving also shows that there was a waterworks tower nearby. This pumped the heavily polluted Thames water into people's houses until the nineteenth century. On the next walk you will see Sir Joseph Bazalgette's bust and hear how he solved the pollution problems by building the embankments.

There is much more to see and explore around these

gardens. Looking up to the right, you see the Adelphi, a 1930s art deco office block, and beyond that the former headquarters of Shell UK with the largest clock face in London on its top storey.

Now walk down the steps to the left of the watergate and continue along the path that leads to Villiers Street. On your right, you will pass Gordon's Wine Bar, a favourite locale of Rudyard Kipling, who lived briefly next door in Villiers Street (the house has a plaque). Turn left down Villiers Street and pass through Embankment Underground Station. On the other side of the station you will find some steps that take you up the footbridge, called the Golden Jubilee Bridge, attached to Hungerford Railway Bridge.

13. GOLDEN JUBILEE BRIDGE

Brunel, whose statue we saw by Somerset House, built a suspension bridge here in 1845 to allow people to cross the river from the south to Hungerford Market. The market was removed when Charing Cross Railway Station was built in 1864 and the present nine-span wrought iron lattice girder railway bridge replaced Brunel's bridge. The chains from Hungerford Bridge were reused for Brunel's famous Clifton Bridge over the River Severn in Bristol. The two footbridges, on either side of the railway, with their white fan-like supports, were officially opened by the Queen in 2003 as the Golden Jubilee Bridge.

To the south of the river you will see the South Bank cultural centre. The Royal Festival Hall is nearest to Hungerford Bridge. This was built in 1951 for the Festival of Britain and is the only building left from that time. Later structures in the concrete New Brutalist style house the Queen Elizabeth Concert Hall, the Hayward Art Gallery and, on the other side of Waterloo Bridge, the National Theatre. Plans are constantly being made to beautify the area, but so far we are left with the concrete blocks which many feel do not do justice to their exciting interiors. On the north side of the river you have a view of the buildings you have just passed. Above the railway line behind you is Terry Farrell's post-modern Embankment Place, constructed in 1990. This is mainly occupied by the accountancy firm, PricewaterhouseCoopers.

The walk ends here. Either return to Embankment Underground Station, or walk across the footbridge and you will eventually come to Waterloo Station.

Whitehall, Westminster and Lambeth

START: Embankment Underground Station (Embankment exit).
   Walk to your right along the Embankment under Hungerford
   Bridge. When you reach the far side of the bridge, turn right
   and walk up the steps onto Golden Jubilee Bridge.
FINISH: Lambeth Palace.
WALKING DISTANCE: 2 miles
HIGHLIGHTS: Whitehall Palace remains, Big Ben, Houses of
   Parliament, St Margaret's Church, Westminster Abbey,
   Rodin's *Burghers of Calais*, Lambeth Palace, Museum of
   Garden History.
FOOD & DRINK: Apart from street snack bars, there is nowhere
   to eat on the direct route until the café in the Museum of
   Garden History towards the end.

This walk covers the great palaces of the monarchs and the
archbishops of Canterbury. Little is left of Whitehall Palace
apart from the Banqueting House, and the name 'Whitehall'
which is still often used to mean 'the Government'. The
Palace of Westminster has now become the Houses of
Parliament which, together with Big Ben, provides one of
the world's most recognisable views. Across the road from
Parliament are two contrasting churches: St Margaret's is the
parish church of the Members of Parliament, with much
fine stained glass and an intimate atmosphere; Westminster
Abbey is where the nation's great ecclesiastical ceremonies
take place. Further on you come to Victoria Tower Gardens
with views across the river and Rodin's *Burghers of Calais*
sculpture. After a detour to see the idiosyncratic St John's,
Smith Square, you cross the river to the Borough of
Lambeth. Here you have superb views of the Houses of
Parliament, as well as the medieval Lambeth Palace and the
Church of St Mary-at-Lambeth, now converted into the
Museum of Garden History.

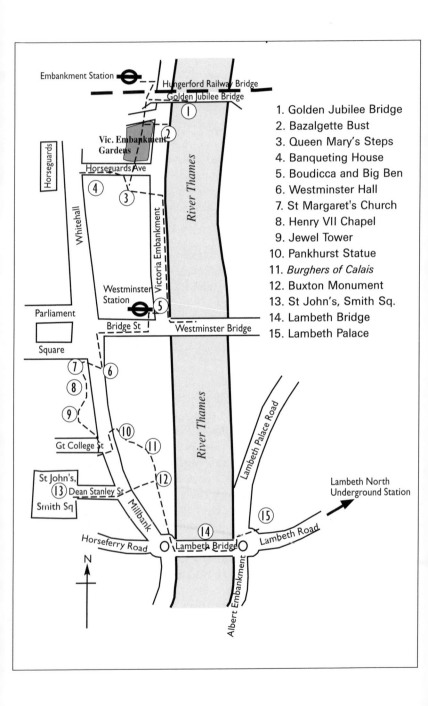

Embankment Station

Hungerford Railway Bridge
Golden Jubilee Bridge
①

Vic. Embankment
Gardens
②

Horseguards Ave

Horseguards

④

Whitehall

③

Victoria Embankment

River Thames

Westminster
Station
⑤

Parliament

Bridge St

Westminster Bridge

Square

⑦
⑥
⑧
⑨

Gt College St
⑩
⑪

⑫

St John's,
⑬ Dean Stanley St
Smith Sq

Millbank

River Thames

Lambeth Palace Road

Lambeth North
Underground Station

⑮

Horseferry Road

Lambeth Bridge
⑭

Lambeth Road

Albert Embankment

N

1. Golden Jubilee Bridge
2. Bazalgette Bust
3. Queen Mary's Steps
4. Banqueting House
5. Boudicca and Big Ben
6. Westminster Hall
7. St Margaret's Church
8. Henry VII Chapel
9. Jewel Tower
10. Pankhurst Statue
11. *Burghers of Calais*
12. Buxton Monument
13. St John's, Smith Sq.
14. Lambeth Bridge
15. Lambeth Palace

1. GOLDEN JUBILEE BRIDGE

The last walk, Blackfriars, Temple and Embankment, finished with the view downstream from the Golden Jubilee Bridge, and I recommend you start this one by mounting the upstream footbridge to have a look at where this walk will take you. On the South Bank is the London Eye, constructed in 2000. It was meant to be ready for the Millennium but its opening was delayed due to various problems. The first attempt to raise it from its prone position stretching halfway across the river failed. For a day it leant precariously at an angle of 45 degrees over the Thames, providing one of the most exciting views in London. Now it has become a must for every visitor to London and it is impossible to believe it will not outlast its original five-year lifespan. Next to the London Eye is the early twentieth-century County Hall, the former headquarters of the Greater London Council. This institution was abolished by Margaret Thatcher in the 1980s partly because she did not approve of its leader, Ken Livingstone. Tony Blair restored the institution in 2001, albeit in a slimmed-down format. The first Mayor to be elected was none other than Ken Livingstone, although he was not allowed back into County Hall as this is now a mixed-use building, housing the Marriott Hotel, the London Aquarium, and the Salvador Dali and Saatchi art galleries.

On the North Bank, where you will be walking, is the continuation of Victoria Embankment Gardens. The extravagant French Renaissance-style building by the gardens is Whitehall Court, built in 1884 as a hotel and apartment block. Beyond that is the Ministry of Defence and the Norman Shaw Building, both of which you will see close up later. Westminster Bridge is next upstream, and beyond are the Houses of Parliament.

Descend again to street level. Cross to the river side of the Embankment. Just upstream of the Hungerford Railway Bridge you will come to George Simond's decorative bust of Sir Joseph Bazalgette.

2. BAZALGETTE BUST

The bust shows the face of Sir Joseph Bazalgette, who was responsible for the most impressive engineering works in the history of London, but is not as famous as he should be as much of it is invisible. By the middle of the nineteenth century, over 250,000 houses emptied their sewage into the River Thames following the widespread use of the newly improved water closet. Much of London's drinking water was also pumped from the Thames, thus causing frequent cholera and dysentery epidemics. Despite lobbying by social and medical reformers, nothing was done until 1858, when the pollution was such that the Members of Parliament, sitting upstream in Westminster, could not bear the smell. The year was named the Year of the Great Stink, and they at last decided to take drastic action. Sir Joseph Bazalgette was commissioned to build the Thames embankments under which he constructed intercepting sewers. These trapped the entire sewage outflow and took it downstream to the east of London.

Under the Embankment he also incorporated tunnels for the new District Line Underground Railway, as well as a tunnel for gas and water pipes. His other projects

Sir Joseph Bazalgette, whose sewers rescued London from pollution in the nineteenth century

included the construction of bridges at Hammersmith and Battersea, and the introduction of hundreds of London plane trees along the Embankment and elsewhere. Originally introduced in the sixteenth century, these trees have the ability to survive in big city pollution by shedding their bark, as can be seen from their mottled trunks. They also raise the amount of oxygen in the air.

Cross back over the Embankment by the nearest pedestrian crossing into Victoria Embankment Gardens. Continue through the gardens and at the end cross over Horseguards Avenue. Here you find yourself by some ruined steps at the corner of the Ministry of Defence, the massive white-stone building that fronts this part of the gardens.

3. QUEEN MARY'S STEPS

This was the new landing stage built for Queen Mary by Sir Christopher Wren in 1695, and is one of the few visible remains of the great palace of Whitehall. The original palace had been built for Cardinal Wolsey in the early sixteenth century. It was so grand that it outshone the outmoded Palace of Westminster belonging to Henry VIII. Wolsey fell out of favour because he failed to gain the Pope's agreement to annul Henry's marriage to Catherine of Aragon. While being entertained at Whitehall by Cardinal Wolsey, Henry posed the question 'Of what use to a man of the cloth is such luxury?' Wolsey had no answer and decided it was safest to give his palace to the King. The palace was extended and improved by a succession of monarchs until most of it was burned down in 1698.

Walk away from the river to the end of Horseguards Avenue.

4. BANQUETING HOUSE

The most impressive remaining building of the Palace of Whitehall is the Banqueting House. The architect was Inigo Jones, who built it for King James I in the Palladian style. Inside you can see Rubens' great ceiling paintings, commissioned by Charles I to celebrate the benefits of wise (Stuart) rule. One of the most famous events in British history took place on a platform outside the front of this building – the execution of the same Charles I on the order of Oliver Cromwell. If you have time it is well worth paying the admission charge to see inside.

Look across the road called Whitehall at Horse Guards, where two mounted troopers of the Queen's Household Cavalry are posted from 10 a.m. to 4 p.m. daily. This picturesque guard house was designed by the architect William Kent in 1758. Look closely at the clock at the top of the central gateway arch and you will see a black blob at the two o'clock mark. This represents the exact hour when Charles I was executed on 30 January 1649.

Now retrace your steps to the Embankment. Cross over it at the nearest pedestrian crossing and go down to the side of the river. Walk along the riverbank until you come to the steps leading up to Westminster Bridge.

5. BOUDICCA AND BIG BEN

The statue, sculpted by Hamo Thorneycroft in the 1850s, shows the Ancient British Queen Boudicca in her war chariot. She was queen of the most powerful native tribe, the Iceni, who were relatively friendly with the Roman conquerors of Britain. When her husband died in AD 60, the Romans made the mistake of degrading her and raping her daughters. She raised an army, killed as many Romans as she could and burned down Roman London. Eventually she was defeated by the full Roman Army, which had been fighting in the north of England.

Looking up at the statue and at Big Ben behind it provides one of the really spectacular views in London. Big Ben itself is actually the name of the bell inside the clock tower. It was named after Sir Benjamin Hall, the Chief Commissioner of Works at the time, or possibly after the popular boxer, Benjamin Caunt, who had just fought a bout of 60 rounds. It was cast in the Whitechapel

Queen Boudicca in her chariot, seemingly
about to attack Big Ben

Bell Foundry in the East End of London in 1858, and
weighs nearly 14 tons. The minute hands on the clock
faces are as tall as a London bus. Since 1923 its chimes
have been broadcast on the BBC to herald the New Year.
It is possible to climb up the stairs as far as the clock face,
where you can see Big Ben itself. However you need to
ask a local MP in order to arrange a visit.

The original Westminster Bridge was opened in 1753.
Until that time, London Bridge was the only way of
crossing the Thames except for the many ferries. When
the bridge was opened, Parliament had to pay
compensation to the Archbishop of Canterbury, who
owned the horse ferry at Lambeth Palace, as well as to the
watermen who ran it. It was on the original Westminster
Bridge that William Wordsworth wrote his sonnet, with its
famous opening lines:

> Earth hath not anything to show more fair.
> Dull must he be of mind who can pass by
> A sight so touching in its majesty.

The view has changed over the 200 years that have passed since these lines were written, but it is still inspiring. The bridge too has changed as it became unstable, and in 1864 had to be replaced by the present seven-arch cast-iron bridge, designed by Charles Barry, the architect of the Houses of Parliament.

Walk up the steps and turn left. Go to the middle of Westminster Bridge to see the modern version of Wordsworth's majestic view. Under the central lamppost you will find a plaque with the full version of his sonnet. Return to cross Bridge Street by the pedestrian crossing. Go past Big Ben towards Parliament Square, where you turn left and walk past the guarded entrance to the House of Commons to the statue of Oliver Cromwell, standing with his bible in one hand and a sword in the other in front of Westminster Hall.

6. WESTMINSTER HALL

The statue of Oliver Cromwell is also by Hamo Thorneycroft. Cromwell overthrew the monarchy and to many is the hero of Parliamentary democracy in this country. However he is a controversial hero, and when the statue was erected in 1899, the Irish Members of Parliament managed to stop payment for the statue. The Prime Minister, Lord Rosebery, had to pay for it out of his own pocket. If you look across the road, you will see a bust of a bearded man over the door of St Margaret's Church. This is the head of Charles I, whom Cromwell had executed. They stare at each other for all eternity.

Behind Cromwell is Westminster Hall, the oldest remaining part of the Palace of Westminster. It was built by William II in the eleventh century, but largely reconstructed in the fourteenth century by Henry Yevele for Richard II. The Hall served as the main law court in England until the nineteenth century and many famous trials have occurred here, including those of Charles I and Sir Thomas More.

Now cross the road by the pedestrian crossing and enter St Margaret's Church, if it is not closed for a service.

7. ST MARGARET'S CHURCH

The present church dates from 1523 and was made the parish church of the House of Commons in 1614. At the front on the right side is the Speaker's pew. John Milton's and Winston Churchill's weddings took place in St Margaret's, and William Caxton and Walter Raleigh are buried here.

The chief glory of the church is its stained glass. The great East Window dates from the early sixteenth century. At the bottom on the left it depicts the kneeling Henry VIII and on the right his first wife, Catherine of Aragon. In the centre of the north aisle wall is a fragment of nineteenth-century stained glass, showing the printer William Caxton demonstrating his new printing press to King Edward IV. At the west end on the north side is a window celebrating the life and works of John Milton, and in the centre over the entrance a window donated by the State of Virginia in honour of Sir Walter Raleigh and also featuring Queen Elizabeth I. A very different style of stained glass adorns the south aisle wall. This was designed in 1967 by John Piper and installed by Patrick Rentgens.

Walk on past the Henry VII Chapel which forms the east end of Westminster Abbey and go into the open grassed area to the right.

8. HENRY VII CHAPEL

The Henry VII Chapel was built in the sixteenth century in the Perpendicular style. It is interesting to compare this with the plainer Early English Gothic style of most of the rest of Westminster Abbey, which dates from the thirteenth and fourteenth centuries. Look across the road at the Houses of Parliament, which were built in the nineteenth century in Yorkshire limestone by the architect Charles Barry and the Gothic expert Augustus Pugin. You will notice that the architectural style is almost indistinguishable from that of the Henry VII Chapel.

From the time of the Saxon King Edward the Confessor, who moved his palace from the area of the City of London to Westminster in the eleventh century, there have always been both an abbey church and Palace of Westminster here. The palace was no longer lived in by the monarch after Henry VIII moved into Whitehall. Instead it was made the home of Parliament and the Law Courts, though still retaining the name Palace of Westminster even up to today.

Parliament first met in 1295. As today there were two chambers – the Lords and the Commons. The Commons were at the time less important and had no permanent home. Instead they often met in the Chapter House of the abbey, which is the octagonal building you see behind the trees at the back of the grassed area. The monks living in the abbey eventually grew tired of the rowdiness of the sessions and it was a relief to all concerned when Henry VIII's son, Edward VI, gave the Chapel of St Stephen in the palace to the Commons as their permanent home. A great fire consumed most of the ramshackle old Palace of Westminster in 1834, which gave Barry and Pugin the chance to create the world-famous structure you see today. Public tours are currently available during the summer recess, or by asking a local MP.

Continue along the road, which is here known as Old Palace Yard, until you reach the old tower, known as the Jewel Tower, surrounded by a grassy moat.

9. JEWEL TOWER

This tower was built by Henry Yevele, who also reconstructed Westminster Hall, in 1365. It is made of Kentish ragstone, has three storeys and used to be surrounded by a moat where fish could be caught. It was used to store the monarch's jewels, robes, furs and gold vessels. Today it houses an exhibition about the history of Parliament.

Across the road is Victoria Tower, the highest part of the Houses of Parliament. The Queen enters here to deliver her speech at the annual state opening of Parliament. If you see a flag flying on top of the tower, this means that Parliament is in session.

Further along on this side of the road is a sculpture by Henry Moore: *Knife Edge, Two Pieces*. It is a familiar sight on television as interviews with politicians are often conducted in front of it, with a fine view of Parliament behind them.

Walk past the sculpture and across Great College Street until you come to the pedestrian crossing, where you cross over the main road, Millbank, to the river side. Turn back to the left to enter Victoria Tower Gardens.

10. PANKHURST STATUE

This bronze statue was erected in 1930 in honour of Dame Emmeline Pankhurst, the leader of the militant suffragette movement. She famously said: 'The broken pane is today the most potent act in politics.' The bronze medallion of her daughter, Dame Christabel, who fought with her mother for votes for women, was placed here in 1959. On the left of the group is a bronze medallion of the Women's Social and Political Union (WSPU) badge, which was given as a badge of honour to every suffragette who was imprisoned for breaking the law for the sake of the cause.

Women over 30 finally got the vote in 1918. Some say this was more because women showed how effective they could be during the First World War than because of their militancy before the war. Full equality was achieved in 1929 when, with a few exceptions such as peers and criminals, all men and women aged 21 or over could vote. Today the voting age is 18.

Walk on into the gardens and stop at the *Burghers of Calais* statue.

11. *BURGHERS OF CALAIS*

This statue is an identical casting to Rodin's *Burghers of Calais* bronze group in Calais. It was erected here in 1915 as a result of a grant from the National Arts Collection Fund. Unlike the Calais version, which has been allowed to turn a mottled green, this bronze has been covered in black wax. Cognoscenti disapprove of this method, but the stark contrast of the group of blackened figures in chains against the golden yellow Gothic Victoria Tower behind provides yet another stunning sight. The statue will soon be taken away for restoration and this will doubtless involve the removal of the black wax.

The sculpture shows the burghers who surrendered themselves to King Edward III in 1347 in order to save their town from the harsh siege by the English Army. Edward's wife, Phillipa of Hainault, asked him to spare them and he agreed – another triumph for women.

Walk on through the gardens until you come to a rather gaudy Victorian Gothic monument.

12. BUXTON MONUMENT

This is a monument to Sir Thomas Fowell Buxton, one of the leaders of the movement which finally passed the Bill to emancipate all slaves in the British Empire in 1837. He had taken over the leadership of the antislavery party from William Wilberforce in 1824 when the latter had to resign because of ill health. After the Abolition of Slavery Bill was passed and until his death in 1845, he worked on prison reform.

Walk out of the gardens, cross the main road, now called Millbank, and go up Dean Stanley Street to Smith Square.

13. ST JOHN'S, SMITH SQUARE

This extraordinary Baroque church was designed by Thomas Archer in 1713 during the reign of Queen Anne. It is said that he asked her what she wanted it to look like, and that the portly Queen kicked over her footstool so that its four legs were uppermost and said, 'Like that'. Hence it is colloquially known as 'Queen Anne's Footstool'. It contains a wealth of baroque features, including idiosyncratic Venetian windows, broken pediments and huge keystones. Charles Dickens however disliked it intensely and describes it in *Our Mutual Friend* as 'a very hideous church with four towers at the corners, generally resembling some petrified monster, frightful and gigantic, on its back with its legs in the air'. After damage in the Second World War it was deconsecrated and restored as a concert hall. It is sometimes possible to go inside to hear a rehearsal for free.

Now retrace your steps back to Victoria Tower Gardens. Continue to Lambeth Bridge, ascend the steps to the bridge and walk halfway across the river.

14. LAMBETH BRIDGE

Downstream is a splendid view of the river frontage of the Houses of Parliament. On the opposite side of the river next to Westminster Bridge is St Thomas's Hospital. This was moved in the nineteenth century from its original position near London Bridge. It is one of London's premier teaching hospitals and houses the Florence Nightingale Museum of Nursing.

The present Lambeth Bridge was built with five steel arches in 1932 to the design of the architect Sir Reginald Blomfield. It spans the Thames near the location of the horse ferry for which Parliament compensated the Archbishop of Canterbury when Westminster Bridge was built. The approach road is still called Horseferry Road.

Now look upstream away from the Houses of Parliament. In the distance on the left side of the river is a cream and green ziggurat-style building. This is the 1993 Vauxhall Cross, headquarters of MI6, our foreign Secret Service. It has been called the worst-kept secret in London. The architect was Terry Farrell, who also designed Embankment Place. A much better-kept secret is the MI5 building, housing the domestic Secret Service, which is the solid grey structure with a gold roof on the side of the river you have just come from, immediately upstream of Lambeth Bridge.

Carry on over the river, turn left and then cross Lambeth Palace Road.

15. LAMBETH PALACE

The Tudor red-brick gateway in front of you is known as Morton's Gate and is the entrance to Lambeth Palace, the London home of the archbishops of Canterbury. Archbishop Baldwin took over the manor here in the thirteenth century as he realised it was essential to have ready access to the monarch. The palace is of great historical interest, especially when you consider that the Archbishop used to be the second most powerful person in the land. No fewer than four of them were executed or murdered, from Thomas à Becket in 1170 to Thomas Laud in 1640.

Archbishop Morton, who built this fine gateway in 1501, was responsible for collecting taxes for Henry VII. He invented the ingenious method called Morton's Fork. If you entertained him well, he pointed out that you must

Lambeth Palace gatehouse, built by Archbishop Morton in 1501

be rich, so could afford to pay high taxes. When the word got around and people tried entertaining him frugally, he attacked them for being misers who had hidden away their riches and insisted they pay equally high taxes. Thus apparently rich and poor suffered alike.

Next to Lambeth Palace is the former church of St Mary-at-Lambeth, which has a fourteenth-century tower but was largely rebuilt in 1852 by Philip Hardwick. After war damage, the Church Commissioners wanted to sell it off for redevelopment. Fortunately the Tradescant Trust was set up and raised enough money to restore the building as the Museum of Garden History. John Tradescant, who lived nearby in Lambeth Road, was gardener to Charles I. He introduced many new plants from abroad and the perennial flower 'tradescantia' is named after him. As well as many paintings, tools and designs concerned with the history of gardening in this country, there is a small area with plantings typical of Tradescant's time. You can see several imposing tombs here, including that of Tradescant himself and Captain Bligh of the *Bounty*.

You can end the walk with refreshments in the museum café. The museum is a delight, not only for keen gardeners. A donation is requested. You have a ten-minute walk to the nearest railway station. Either go up Lambeth Road and turn left to arrive at Lambeth North Underground Station, or retrace your steps to Westminster Underground Station, or walk along the Albert Embankment to Vauxhall Underground and Mainline Station.

CHAPTER 2

Outer London River Walks

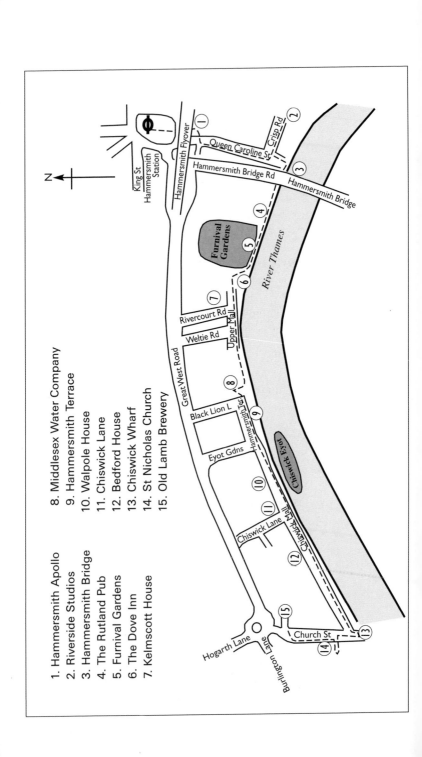

1. Hammersmith Apollo
2. Riverside Studios
3. Hammersmith Bridge
4. The Rutland Pub
5. Furnival Gardens
6. The Dove Inn
7. Kelmscott House
8. Middlesex Water Company
9. Hammersmith Terrace
10. Walpole House
11. Chiswick Lane
12. Bedford House
13. Chiswick Wharf
14. St Nicholas Church
15. Old Lamb Brewery

Hammersmith and Chiswick

START: Hammersmith Underground Station (follow the signs to
the exit to Queen Caroline Street by the Apollo Cinema).
FINISH: Hogarth roundabout – the nearest Underground is
Turnham Green and the nearest mainline station is Chiswick.
WALKING DISTANCE: 2 miles
HIGHLIGHTS: Hammersmith Bridge, The Dove Inn, Kelmscott,
Fullers, Smith & Turner Brewery, St Nicholas Church and
churchyard, Hogarth House.
FOOD & DRINK: The Rutland pub, The Blue Anchor pub, The
Dove Inn, The Black Lion pub, Mawson's Arms.

People travelling by car along the busy Great Western
Road must find it hard to envisage the two delightful
villages that still hug the river just out of sight. You will
start the walk with the deafening noise of Hammersmith
Flyover. Soon you leave the noise behind as you walk to
Bazalgette's decorative Hammersmith Bridge. You now
walk along the side of the river past several attractive
riverside houses and historic pubs until you reach
Kelmscott, the former London home of William Morris.
Soon after this, Hammersmith becomes Chiswick. The
houses here are even more exclusive despite the
sometimes powerful smell emanating from the brewery.
Near the end you come to the Parish Church of St
Nicholas, where William Hogarth is buried. His former
house is nearby and can be visited without charge.

1. HAMMERSMITH APOLLO
The most noticeable feature here is the flyover, built in
1961 by the London County Council to improve the
increasingly heavy traffic flow between London and the
west. This is a prime example of how the automobile can
ruin the environment. The name Hammersmith comes

from the words 'hammer' and 'smithy' from medieval times. The noise of the smith's hammer has been replaced by that of the car and the lorry, but probably people around here have got used to noise by now.

The parish church of St Paul's stands isolated just by the flyover. It was built in 1887 in the Gothic style. William Tierney Clarke, who built the first Hammersmith Bridge, is buried here. To the east you can see a modern glass office block shaped like Noah's Ark. This is in fact called The Ark, designed in 1991 by Ralph Erskine. It has a number of environmental features, including an air-conditioning system that circulates a supply of fresh air while the stale air is discharged through ventilators in the atrium roof. Triple glazing reduces heat loss and helps protect staff from traffic noise from the flyover. Unfortunately it initially caused problems for local inhabitants as the noise from passing vehicles evidently reverberated even louder off the glass walls.

Now walk down Queen Caroline Street, turn left at Crisp Road, and in about 100 metres you will find Riverside Studios on your right.

2. RIVERSIDE STUDIOS

The Riverside Studios are an avant-garde media and artistic centre. Inside are three auditoriums, including an art gallery which specialises in contemporary art exhibitions. Riverside Studios play host to theatre, dance, cinema and film production, and if you need to recover from standing under Hammersmith Flyover there is a small café.

Retrace your steps to Queen Caroline Street, then turn down towards the river and stand on the terrace near Hammersmith Bridge.

3. HAMMERSMITH BRIDGE

William Tierney Clarke built the first suspension bridge in London here in 1827. He was also responsible for the bridge over the Thames at Marlow, and for the famous Chain Bridge over the Danube in Budapest. The present impressively decorative bridge was built in 1887 by Sir Joseph Bazalgette, who reused the old piers and abutments from the original bridge. In 1919 Lt Campbell dived into the river to save a woman who tried to commit suicide. She was saved, but he died. A plaque on the bridge commemorates his bravery. The Real IRA has twice tried to blow up the bridge, the first time in 2000, but it has survived despite having to be closed for over a year on the second occasion.

The large red-brick structure to the left across the river is Harrods Depository, now converted into expensive apartments. Beyond is Wetlands which used to be a large reservoir but is now a bird sanctuary. The reservoir became redundant once the Thames Ring Main was constructed, as this can supply enough water from the large reservoirs upstream at Staines.

Walk under the bridge and carry on along the riverside path, known here as Lower Mall. Note the river walls, which have had to be heightened to avoid flooding at high tide.

The distinctive towers and suspension chains of Hammersmith Bridge

73

4. THE RUTLAND PUB

The two pubs here, The Rutland and The Blue Anchor, have interesting pictures of old Hammersmith and of the Oxford and Cambridge Boat Race, which reaches its half-way point at Hammersmith Bridge. Crowds throng to the bridge to watch the boats speed underneath. By now it is usually obvious who will win the race, but in 2003 Cambridge were leading at this point, only to be surprisingly overtaken by the less-favoured Oxford crew. Overall, up to 2003, the race tally is Cambridge 77, Oxford 71, with one draw in 1877. The Rutland dates from the nineteenth century and used to have three storeys, but lost the top storey after being hit by a bomb in the Second World War. The other pub, The Blue Anchor, dates from 1722. It was used during the filming of *Sliding Doors*, starring Gwyneth Paltrow.

Lower Mall houses date mainly from the eighteenth century. This is now a conservation area, so the owners cannot alter them. It is hard to see why they would want to, as they are so attractive as they are, with their fanlights and balconies overlooking this beautiful stretch of the river. In 2001, Beach House was sold for £2.25 million. The family had originally paid £8,000 for it in 1955.

Go on along Lower Mall until you come to an open grassy area.

5. FURNIVAL GARDENS

The gardens are named after Dr Furnival, a nineteenth-century social reformer. They are sited where Hammersmith started as a small village in medieval times. There used to be a creek here, which was navigable by barges as far up as King Street to the north of the Great West Road. Today it is covered over as an overflow sewer. If you look over the river wall you can see where it still flows into the Thames. Beyond this is Hammersmith Pier, which survives from the days when there was a harbour here.

Having walked to the far end of the gardens, go through the narrow passage at the back of The Dove Inn. At the end of the passage look back at the inn.

6. THE DOVE INN

There has been an inn on this site since the seventeenth century, but the present building dates from the eighteenth century. Many famous people have enjoyed its hospitality, as can be seen from pictures hanging on the walls. During the nineteenth century the name was changed to 'The Doves', but has now reverted to the original 'Dove'. When asked why the plural was used, the landlord explains that after spending an evening drinking here, you are likely to see at least two doves when looking up at the sign. The beer garden overlooking the river gives splendid views over to Hammersmith Bridge.

In the passage just before the Dove you will have seen a plaque to T.J. Cobden Sanderson. He was a colleague of William Morris, whose house you will come to shortly. Morris adopted the Arts & Crafts style synonymous with free craftsmanship. After his death, Sanderson and Emery Walker set up the Doves Press to carry on producing the work of Morris's Kelmscott Press in the Arts & Crafts style. In fact it was Sanderson who invented the name 'arts & crafts'. Sanderson's own name is commemorated in the famous wallpaper firm.

Just along the road, which is now called Upper Mall, is Kelmscott House on the right-hand side

7. KELMSCOTT HOUSE

This substantial five-bay, three-storeyed house was built in 1780. Sir Francis Ronalds lived here in 1816 when he invented the electric telegraph and sent signals along eight miles of wires in his garden here. Unfortunately the Admiralty, to whom Ronalds offered the invention, said they could not see any use for it. It was only much later in the century that cables were laid all over the world and the telegraph became the fastest mode of communication at the time. A plaque over the coach-house door records Ronalds's achievement.

In 1878, William Morris took over the house and renamed it after his Oxfordshire home, which was also on the Thames. He would often row with his friends and family between the two houses. Despite his wealthy family background, he became more and more radical in his political outlook. After becoming disillusioned with the Liberals, he formed the Socialist League and later the Hammersmith Socialist Society which met in the coach house here.

Today the main house of Kelmscott is privately owned. The basement and coach house are the headquarters of the William Morris Society, which has set up a museum about his life. Here you can see examples of his work in textile and wallpaper design as well as his actual printing press, on which were printed 66 volumes, mainly using his own typeface designs.

Continue along Upper Mall until you come to a garden with a brick arcaded wall, behind which is The Black Lion pub.

8. MIDDLESEX WATER COMPANY

This was one of the many water companies that used to supply water from the Thames. Now all the water is supplied from reservoirs upstream in the Staines area. You will also see a plaque to William Tierney Clarke, who was the chief engineer of the first Hammersmith Bridge.

Walk past the pub into Hammersmith Terrace.

9. HAMMERSMITH TERRACE

The 17 substantial houses here were built in the 1750s. They all have gardens on the other side facing the river. They are not as symmetrical as typical Georgian houses, and some of the Doric stucco porches are painted black.

Several of the houses have plaques: Edward Johnston, calligrapher and teacher of the sculptor Eric Gill, lived in No. 3; Sir Emery Walker, the expert on printing typefaces and a colleague of William Morris and T.J. Cobden Sanderson, lived in No. 7; A.P. Herbert lived for 50 years in No. 12. He was Member of Parliament for Oxford University until the seat was abolished in 1950. He is best known for his novel, *The Water Gypsies*, which is set on the Thames, and for his humorous *Misleading Cases in the Common Law*. One case involved an angry customer who presented his bank a cheque written on a cow.

Go to the end of the Terrace and on into Chiswick Mall. This is the boundary between the two villages. Carry on until you reach Walpole House.

10. WALPOLE HOUSE

This imposing house, built in the early 1700s, is named after the Walpole family who owned it. Sir Robert Walpole was Britain's first Prime Minister. Thomas, his nephew, lived here and is buried in St Nicholas Church which you will see later. William Thackeray attended a school here in 1817 and is thought to have used it as a model for Miss Pinkerton's Academy in his novel *Vanity Fair*. Becky Sharp and her friend Amelia attend a school in Chiswick in a stately old brick house. Becky is treated as an inferior by Miss Pinkerton as she is from a lower class than the rest of the girls. When they both finally leave the school, the one kindly teacher gives Becky a dictionary. Becky returns the favour by throwing the dictionary out of the window of the departing coach. Next door is Strawberry House, built at the same time, but with an attractive iron porch added in the 1790s.

The island in the river nearby is called Chiswick Eyot. This is pronounced 'eight' and is an old Saxon word for island that is commonly used for the islands in the Thames. Osiers grow on it and used to be cut for baskets for fishing in former times. Unfortunately the island is being washed away. It has shrunk from 1,200 metres in 1900 to 300 metres today. At low tide it is possible to walk across to it. At high tide the water can come right up on to the road, so that it becomes impassable.

Walk along until you come to Chiswick Lane on the right.

11. CHISWICK LANE

There was an old draw dock here where boats could be moored and dragged up the slope onto dry land. On the far corner of Chiswick Lane is Belle Vue cottage, the traditional home of the chief brewer of Fuller, Smith and Turner's Brewery. If you make a short detour up Chiswick Lane you will see the brewery entrance, and just beyond that, The Mawson's Arms pub. Thomas Mawson founded the brewery in 1701, but it was taken over by Fuller, Smith and Turner in the nineteenth century.

Continue along Chiswick Mall to Bedford House.

12. BEDFORD HOUSE

This house originally belonged to Edward Russell, the younger son of Earl Russell whom you will meet shortly as the builder of a wall by St Nicholas Church. Russell is the family name of the earls and dukes of Bedford. They own the freehold of large parts of Bloomsbury, where Russell Square is the largest of the many squares in the area. The house was rebuilt in the eighteenth century and has been split into two, now called Bedford and Eynham. The actor Michael Redgrave lived here from 1945 to 1954.

Further on is the present vicarage and, after that, the old vicarage, built in 1658 but re-fronted in the eighteenth century with a fine bow window. This is the last house on Chiswick Mall.

Walk to the end of the road and stop at the stone causeway that slopes down to the river.

13. CHISWICK WHARF

This was the old slipway from which a ferry operated from 1659 until the 1930s. It is still used as a dock for unloading timber and hops for the brewery and osiers cut from Chiswick Eyot.

The modern development to the west of the wharf, called Fisherman's Place, used to be fishermen's cottages until pollution drove the fish away in the nineteenth century. Beyond that, Thorneycroft's Shipyard used to build boats until it moved to Southampton in 1909. The firm's founder was the son of the sculptor, Hamo Thorneycroft, who lived in the house called Greenash on Chiswick Mall. In his garden he kept the plaster of Paris model for his Boudicca statue on Westminster Bridge.

Walk up Church Street and enter the churchyard gate on your left.

The Thames flooding Chiswick Mall to the delight of a family of Canada Geese

14. ST NICHOLAS CHURCH

A church has been on this site since 1181 but the earliest remaining structure is the fifteenth-century tower, built of

Kentish ragstone. The rest of the church had to be rebuilt in the nineteenth century. The architect was J.L. Pearson, who designed it in the same Perpendicular style as the tower.

Many fine memorials are to be found in the churchyard. The large monument with the urn on top surrounded by railings is the tomb of William Hogarth and his wife and family. The famous actor, David Garrick, wrote the fulsome epitaph. Hogarth is best known today for his series of satirical paintings such as *The Rake's Progress* and *Marriage à la Mode*. He lived and worked in London, but spent his last years nearby in Hogarth House. You might like to visit it at the end of the walk – free but a donation is requested.

When you go back out of the churchyard into Church Street, look at the stone tablet on the churchyard wall facing the road. You can with difficulty read the singular inscription about the Earl of Bedford who built the wall to protect the bodies in the churchyard from 'violating of swine and other profanation'. This was the same earl who, with the architect Inigo Jones, developed Covent Garden in the new Palladian style in the seventeenth century.

William Hogarth's tomb in the churchyard of St Nicholas

Continue about 200 metres up Church Street to Mawson Lane, which is the first turning on the right.

15. OLD LAMB BREWERY

A little way along the lane you can see the bell tower of another brewery which operated here from 1790 to 1950. It has been converted into private dwellings. On either side of the lane were two pubs which have also been converted into houses. Lamb Cottage was known as The Lamb Tap and The Old Burlington was The Burlington Arms. The latter is the oldest house in Chiswick, dating from the sixteenth century with its half-timber Elizabethan construction.

Now walk up to the top of Church Street to the Hogarth roundabout, where you can decide what to do next. There is a pub a short way along Burlington Lane to your left. You could visit Chiswick House, which is about 300 metres further along Burlington Lane on your right. You could also visit Hogarth House – you should go under the underpass to Hogarth Lane and you will find it about 400 metres along on your left. Public transport is not very convenient. You can carry on along Burlington Lane past Chiswick House and follow the signs to Chiswick Mainline Station, which is a ten-minute walk. The nearest Underground station is Turnham Green, which is also a ten-minute walk on the other side of the Great West Road. Go up Devonshire Road, cross Chiswick High Road, then go up Turnham Green Terrace to the station.

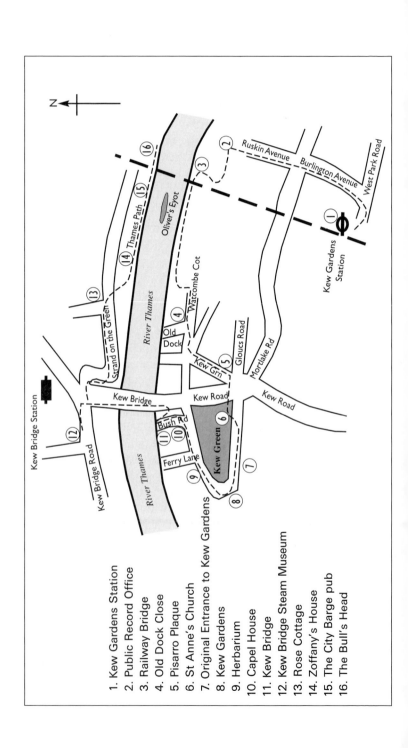

1. Kew Gardens Station
2. Public Record Office
3. Railway Bridge
4. Old Dock Close
5. Pisarro Plaque
6. St Anne's Church
7. Original Entrance to Kew Gardens
8. Kew Gardens
9. Herbarium
10. Capel House
11. Kew Bridge
12. Kew Bridge Steam Museum
13. Rose Cottage
14. Zoffany's House
15. The City Barge pub
16. The Bull's Head

Kew and Strand on the Green

START: Kew Gardens Station. Exit the station from the platform where the trains from London stop. You need to cross under the railway if you arrive from the opposite direction.

FINISH: The Bull's Head, Strand on the Green – the nearest station is Kew Bridge Station.

WALKING DISTANCE: 2 miles

HIGHLIGHTS: Public Record Office, St Anne's Church, Kew Gardens, Kew Bridge Steam Museum, eighteenth-century riverside houses at Strand on the Green.

FOOD & DRINK: Public Record Office cafeteria, ASK restaurant, Café Rouge, The City Barge and The Bull's Head pubs.

Kew is most famous for the Royal Botanic Gardens, however the walker will also find many unexpected delights both around Kew Green and along the riverside. The first surprise on this walk is the vast modern building which now houses the Public Record Office. St Anne's Church on Kew Green is an idiosyncratic mixture of Byzantine and classical styles. The tomb of Thomas Gainsborough is in the churchyard. The Green retains its old village atmosphere: fine eighteenth-century houses, many with royal connections, surround its perimeter, and cricket has been played here for over 250 years. Over the other side of the river you will find the Kew Bridge Steam Museum with its dramatic tall tower, visible for miles around. Finally, you will walk along the Strand on the Green riverside path past houses bedecked with mimosa trees, wisteria and vines, and arrive at two historic pubs.

1. KEW GARDENS STATION
The station was opened in 1869 and resulted in the village of Kew turning into a suburb of London. Until then it was mainly a fishing village as implied by the name, which

comes from an Anglo-Saxon word meaning 'quay'. However, change was inevitable because so many visitors were already flocking to the Botanic Gardens, and the river was becoming polluted. The first part of the walk will take you along suburban roads where Kew's mild climate allows date palms and other exotic plants to grow.

Starting on the side of the station where the trains from London arrive – this is on the opposite side to the ticket office – walk 10 metres along West Park Road and then turn left up Burlington Avenue. At the junction, cross the main road by the pedestrian crossing, and continue up Ruskin Avenue until you arrive at the entrance to the Public Record Office building.

2. PUBLIC RECORD OFFICE

Popularly known as Fort Ruskin, this building was opened in 1977 after it was decided to move the Public Record Office out of the Victorian building in Chancery Lane, which is now the library of King's College. Although the new building looks rather formidable, it is beautifully landscaped with ponds and fountains. Herons and swans are often to be seen, and the lack of pigeons is due to the regular visit of a man with his hawk who is employed for this purpose.

The Public Record Office stores vast numbers of official documents dating back as far as the eleventh-century Domesday Book. It is mainly used for research purposes and members of the public can obtain a reader's pass to do their own research here. There is also a visitor centre where original documents and modern graphical explanations of them are displayed. The exhibition is constantly changing, but the Domesday Book and a version of Magna Carta are usually on display. The Magna Carta was signed by King John in 1216 on the Thames at Runneymede about 15 miles upstream from here. Several later versions were produced and the one on display dates from the reign of King John's successor, Henry III. The exhibition is free, so go in by the front entrance.

Water features and a swan soften the stark, modern architecture of the Public Record Office

Leave the building the same way you came in and walk to your right past the artificial pond, keeping to the right-hand pathway. At the end you will come to an iron gate, which can be opened. Pass through and walk to the right until you reach the river.

3. RAILWAY BRIDGE

The area by the bridge has been left to grow wild, however new apartments are being constructed, so the atmosphere will probably change over the next few years. The bridge takes the Silverlink and District Line trains to London and is noisy. The pub across the river, The Bull's Head, is where the walk will end. To your right the Thames Path leads to an industrial estate, sewage works, rubbish dump, crematorium and finally to Mortlake Brewery. This walk, you will be glad to hear, continues to the left.

Walk to the left along the river path, pass under the bridge and when you come to the end of the allotments, turn sharp left up a narrow passage to Watcombe Cottages. Go up this short road until you reach the end of the terraced cottages.

4. OLD DOCK CLOSE

There used to be a creek here and a dock where fishing boats landed their catches. The creek was covered over in the nineteenth century because of increasing pollution and then the row of cottages was built. The modern development on the right past Old Dock Close is called Westerley Ware after a weir constructed in the creek by local fishermen.

Continue on past the pond on your left until you reach Kew Green. Keeping the pond on your left, walk along the side of the Green until you come to Gloucester Road on your left.

5. PISARRO PLAQUE

Note the Victorian houses bordering this side of the Green, with their delicate terracotta mouldings. Kew was always a favourite place for artists to live and work, and you will see two blue plaques on these houses. The plaque on No. 22 is to Arthur Hughes, a minor Pre-Raphaelite painter, and the one on the end house of Gloucester Road is to Emile Pisarro, the French Impressionist. He stayed here in 1892 and painted several Kew scenes.

Now cross the main road and head for the church on the other side.

6. ST ANNE'S CHURCH

Kew was not big enough to be a parish until 1770, but the inhabitants wanted their own church, so they petitioned Queen Anne to allow them to build one. She gave her permission and £100 towards the cost. The church was completed in 1714 and was dedicated to St Anne, presumably to honour Queen Anne herself. It is an unusual mixture of Byzantine and classical styles in yellow brick and with arched windows.

In the churchyard are several interesting tombs of artists. On the south-west side of the church, surrounded by railings, you will see the tomb of Thomas

Gainsborough and his family. He never actually lived in Kew, but often stayed here with his friend, Joshua Kirby. Gainsborough's portrait of Joshua Kirby and his wife hangs in the National Gallery. At the east end of the churchyard is the plain rectangular tomb of Johann Zoffany, whose house you will see later across the river in Strand on the Green. He painted *The Last Supper*, using local people for models of the Apostles, and himself as St Peter. The painting was intended to hang in St Anne's, but when people started using the names of the apostles for the local men who acted as their models, the wife of the man who was the model for Judas objected so strongly that it had to be removed. The painting now hangs in St Paul's Church in Brentford.

Leaving the churchyard, cross the road on the south side of Kew Green and walk to the right to the gates in front of No. 47.

7. ORIGINAL ENTRANCE TO KEW GARDENS

The plaque on the right of the gates records that this was the original entrance to the Botanic Gardens. It was in the 1670s that the Capel family started collecting rare trees and plants and thus formed the basis for the later development of pleasure gardens by George II's son Frederick. After Frederick's death in 1751 his wife, Princess Augusta, created a botanical garden with the assistance of Lord Bute who lived in No. 37, the large house with the white portico protruding over the pavement. This and most of the houses around this part of Kew Green date from the eighteenth century.

Many famous architects, botanists and landscape gardeners have been associated with the later development of the gardens: William Chambers built the Chinese Pagoda for Princess Augusta in 1761; Decimus Burton built the celebrated Palm House in 1844; Capability Brown landscaped the whole area in the 1770s; and Sir Joseph Banks made the Botanic Gardens famous by the introduction of many exotic plants from all over the world. In 1840 Queen Victoria, who seemingly had little interest in gardening, gave Kew Gardens to the nation. Since then it has combined the functions of botanical research centre and tourist attraction.

Carry on to the end of Kew Green where the present entrance is located.

8. KEW GARDENS

The beautiful wrought iron gates you see were constructed in the Jacobean style in 1848, soon after Kew Gardens were taken over by the government. They were designed by Decimus Burton, the architect of the Palm House. Pedestrian entrances flank the large double gate which was originally intended for carriages. Looking through the gates, you can see some specimen trees and the orangery on the right-hand side of the pathway. William Chambers designed this long rectangular building with its tall arched windows in 1761. Well within living memory the entrance fee was one penny, but now is a more realistic £7.50. Kew Gardens has been given the status of a World Heritage Site and you can spend a whole day here. If you want to finish the walk you should resist the temptation to go in and plan to return another day.

Carry on round the north side of the Green until you come to the red-brick building with railings in front just before Ferry Lane.

9. HERBARIUM

King George III's younger son, the Duke of Cumberland, lived here. He is known as the Butcher of Culloden, having defeated Bonnie Prince Charlie's forces with considerable brutality at Culloden in Scotland in 1745. Today the Herbarium stores dried specimens of all the world's plants and has a research library. It is not open to the public. Just beyond the building is Ferry Lane which used to lead to the ferry that provided a river crossing to

Brentford. Today it leads to the car park by the north entrance to the Botanic Gardens.

Continue along the north side of the Green to No. 83, called Capel House.

10. CAPEL HOUSE

This house is named after the Capel family who originated the gardens in the seventeenth century. The left side of the red-brick house dates from the late seventeenth century. You can tell this because the wooden window frames are flush with the brick walls. This was forbidden in London after the Building Act of 1709 which made it obligatory to recess window frames behind the brickwork in order to reduce the risk of fire spreading. The right-hand side has been added on later, as you can see by the recessed window frames. The herb garden reminds us of the Capel family's interest in plants.

Cricket has been played here on the Green since the time of King George II's son, Prince Frederick. A match took place in 1737 when the prince captained a side against the Duke of Marlborough's team. Needless to say the prince's side won.

Turn left up Bush Road. No. 7 on the right used to be a ladies' lavatory, but is now a desirable private residence. Carry on until you reach the river.

11. KEW BRIDGE

The first Kew Bridge was built in 1759 by the owner of the ferry, Robert Tunstall. Tolls were charged until 1873 when it came under public control. The present bridge was constructed in 1903 to a design by Sir John Wolfe-Barry, who also erected Tower Bridge. The landing stage for boats downstream to London and upstream to Hampton Court is along the path under the bridge.

Now mount the steps which are set back from the river path on this side of the bridge. This takes you onto Kew Bridge itself. Walk over the river to the north side, cross the main road called Kew Bridge Road and turn left towards the tall tower of Kew Bridge Steam Museum.

12. KEW BRIDGE STEAM MUSEUM

This used to act as a pumping station where massive Cornish beam engines pumped water into west London for over a century. Today water is supplied from reservoirs further upstream in the area around Staines, but you can see many of these Cornish engines in operation every weekend. There is also an exhibition on the history of water supply from Roman times to the modern Thames Ring Main.

Go back to the traffic lights at the end of Kew Bridge and cross over Kew Bridge Road to Strand on the Green. Walk along this road towards the river and then continue to Café Rouge.

Tower of the Kew Bridge
Steam Museum

13. ROSE COTTAGE

Just past Café Rouge is Rose Cottage, once the home of Nancy Mitford, one of the notorious daughters of Baron Rosedale. She was the author of a biography of Mme de Pompadour and invented the now outmoded terms 'U' and 'Non-U' referring to correct language usage and social behaviour. She moved from the centre of London social life to this house after her marriage in the 1930s, and joked that she would have to become an old housewife. Of her sisters, Jessica was a communist, Unity a Nazi, and Diana married the fascist Oswald Mosley. This small painted cottage seems an unlikely setting for such controversial characters.

Just past Rose Cottage, the Thames Path branches to the right of the road. Leave the road here and take this path along the side of the river. Note the high steps up to the houses and the rich variety of architectural styles and vegetation as you walk on to No. 65.

14. ZOFFANY'S HOUSE

The towpath here is frequently flooded, which is why the houses have steps up to the entrance doors, and in some cases iron water barriers. Partly due to this there is a delightful variety of flowers and shrubs including fig, vine, wisteria and mimosa.

No. 65 was the home of Johann Zoffany between 1790 and 1810. It dates from the late seventeenth century with its ornate doorcase and well-defined brickwork. Note also the converted gas lights by the door. Zoffany was a prolific artist and friend of kings, queens, maharajahs and actors, many of whose portraits he painted.

Walk on to The City Barge pub.

15. THE CITY BARGE PUB

This ancient pub was known as The Navigator's Arms until the Lord Mayor moored his ceremonial barge here for the winter in the nineteenth century. It was then renamed The City Barge. See the steel door in front of the bar entrance, which prevents flooding by the spring tides.

Walk under the railway bridge and stop at The Bull's Head pub.

16. THE BULL'S HEAD

This historic pub was where Oliver Cromwell once held a meeting, only to be surprised by Royalist forces. It is said that he managed to escape by a secret passage under the river to the island in the middle of the river, which is therefore known as Oliver's Eyot (pronounced like 'eight'). If the tide is out it is possible to descend onto the riverbed here.

Walkers enjoying a pint outside The Bull's Head, with the tower of the Kew Bridge Steam Museum in the far distance

You may wish to refresh yourself in one of these pubs as there is no immediate access to public transport. The nearest mainline station is Kew Bridge, which you reach by retracing your steps along the Thames Path and then crossing back over Kew Bridge Road and walking a short distance to your right. The nearest Underground station is Gunnersbury. Carry on along the Thames Path past The Bull's Head and turn left up Magnolia Road. Continue over the railway bridge and follow the road to the underpass under the Great West Road. Turn left into Harvard Road, which takes you to the car park by Gunnersbury Underground Station.

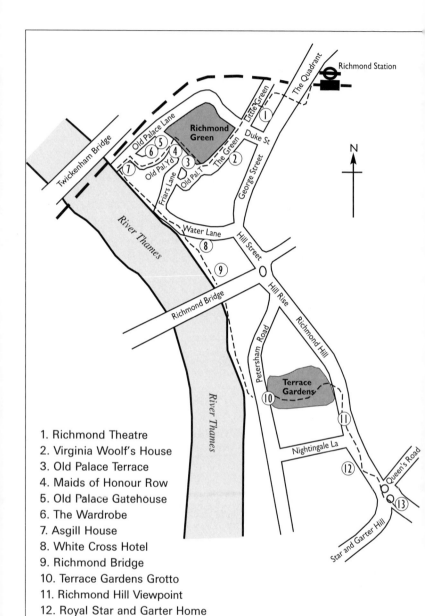

1. Richmond Theatre
2. Virginia Woolf's House
3. Old Palace Terrace
4. Maids of Honour Row
5. Old Palace Gatehouse
6. The Wardrobe
7. Asgill House
8. White Cross Hotel
9. Richmond Bridge
10. Terrace Gardens Grotto
11. Richmond Hill Viewpoint
12. Royal Star and Garter Home
13. Richmond Park

Richmond

START: Richmond Station (this is both a mainline and Underground station. Services are via District Line, Silverlink, or from Waterloo). When you exit the station, turn left and cross the road using the pedestrian crossing. Walk down the narrow passage, which is slightly to your right when you reach the other side. At the end turn into Little Green. Richmond Theatre is about 100 metres further on your left.

FINISH: Richmond Hill – the nearest station is Richmond.

WALKING DISTANCE: 2¼ miles

HIGHLIGHTS: Richmond Green houses, Richmond Palace gateway, Richmond Bridge, Richmond Terrace Gardens, view from Richmond Hill.

FOOD & DRINK: The White Swan and The White Cross pubs, H2O floating restaurant, several hotels at the top of Richmond Hill.

Richmond is one of the very few towns in England to have changed its name in the last 1,000 years. It was originally called Sheen. Then in 1501 Henry VII built his great palace here and he decided to rename the town Richmond after his estates in Richmond, Yorkshire. As you walk across Richmond Green, you find the surprising sight of the gateway to a Tudor palace, and beyond that some more Tudor buildings which formed the palace wardrobe. You then come to the banks of the Thames with attractive pubs, and signs warning of the dangers of flooding. The river scene is framed by the eighteenth-century Richmond Bridge, which is the oldest existing bridge in the London area. After the bridge, you find a grotto which takes you under the main road into the stunningly beautiful Terrace Gardens, with its many exotic trees and flowers. You climb to the top and when you turn round you see one of the most famous views in England, which so impressed a man from Virginia, USA, that he gave the name Richmond to the state capital.

1. RICHMOND THEATRE

Richmond has always been a place of entertainment dating back to the time of Queen Elizabeth I, who enjoyed watching plays here. In the eighteenth century the Theatre Royal was built at the far side of the Green. Many famous actors performed there, including Edmund Kean, who lived in Richmond. He died on stage at the Royal Opera House, Covent Garden, when performing *Othello*. His funeral was in Richmond Church. It was attended by so many people that a friend exclaimed in the middle of the service, 'Bravo, Ned, you've drawn a full house to the last!'

This present theatre was designed by Frank Matcham in 1899. The architecture is a rich mixture of styles and almost a theatrical experience in itself. Inside in the foyer is a ceiling painting showing an image of the building together with various theatrical and mythological figures floating in the sky.

Walk along the west side of the Green. Pass No. 1, which used to have the sign 'Shakespeare House' as it belonged to William Bardolph with whom Shakespeare stayed when performing in front of the Queen. Stop opposite No. 17.

2. VIRGINIA WOOLF'S HOUSE

You will see several early eighteenth-century houses on this side of the Green. No. 11 has an especially fine doorhead. No. 17, built in 1720, was rented by Leonard and Virginia Woolf when they moved from London to Richmond after her mental breakdown. Leonard was fiercely protective of his wife and decided that she would recover more easily by getting away from the hothouse atmosphere of Bloomsbury. He set up the Hogarth Press near here to help keep her occupied and they published 40 books in Richmond before moving back to continue the business in Tavistock Square in Bloomsbury.

Continue to the end of the Green, turn right and stop at Friars Lane.

3. OLD PALACE TERRACE

The row of terraced houses on your left was constructed in 1692 on the site of a demolished manor house. The name 'Friars Lane' denotes the setting up of a friary here by Henry V, only for it to be dissolved 100 years later by Henry VIII. Richard Attenborough owns the house called Friary House to the right of the terrace. He is one of many people in the entertainment business who have chosen to live in Richmond, thus continuing its historical connection with the theatre.

Carry on a little further and stop opposite the tall row of terraced houses with their wrought iron railings and ornamental gates.

4. MAIDS OF HONOUR ROW

These houses have tall sash windows and keystones on the first floor. See also the small iron badge which is a 'fire mark', indicating that the Insurance Company fire engine would be available to put out any fire. If you did not have the appropriate badge, the company would charge exorbitant rates to put out a fire as the owner would have no choice but to pay up. This extortionate system ended in the 1860s with the establishment of the Metropolitan Fire Brigade. The houses are called 'Maids of Honour Row' because they were built in the 1720s for the ladies-in-waiting of George II's wife, Caroline of Anspach.

Walk on until you come to a small road, called Old Palace Road, on the left. Go down this road a short way until you reach the Tudor Gateway.

5. OLD PALACE GATEHOUSE

This is the northern gatehouse of Richmond Palace, built by Henry VII in 1501. At the time it was the showcase of the kingdom, but was eclipsed later on by Hampton Court which Henry VIII preferred, although his daughters, Mary and Elizabeth, often stayed here. Elizabeth died here in 1603 without leaving an heir. She was, however, persuaded to name as her successor James VI of Scotland, the son of Mary Queen of Scots whose death warrant Elizabeth had signed in 1587. Just before Elizabeth died, her royal ring had to be cut from her swollen finger so that a waiting horseman could take it to Scotland to establish James I as the new King of England. Thus ended the Tudor dynasty in England, and the palace then gradually fell into disrepair.

Today you can still see the coat of arms of Henry VII above the centre of the gateway. Also look for the hinges at the side on which the great doors used to hang. The gatehouse is to the left with the typical Tudor diapered brickwork. Further to the left the house known as Old Palace is mainly an eighteenth-century reconstruction in the Tudor manner.

Go through the gateway into the pleasant courtyard.

The Old Palace gatehouse with King Henry VII's coat of arms above the archway

6. THE WARDROBE

You are standing in Old Palace Yard, the great courtyard to the north of the main palace buildings. These were situated by the river through the middle gate where the imposing Trumpeter House now stands. This was built in 1702 soon after the palace was finally demolished. Metternich, the famous Austrian Chancellor, stayed here in 1848 after the many revolutions which shook Europe in that year. He returned to Austria in 1851.

On the left is a row of Tudor houses with more diapered brickwork. The sash windows were installed in the eighteenth century. These were the King's Wardrobe where his private possessions such as jewels and clothes were kept. No. 2 has an armorial stone plaque to George Cave, who was Home Secretary early in the twentieth century, but few have heard of him today.

Walk out of the far end of the courtyard and turn left at Old Palace Lane. Carry on to the banks of the river, noting the plaque at the end of the wall on your left which records brief information about the Old Palace.

7. ASGILL HOUSE

This imposing residence was built in 1760 by the architect, Robert Taylor, for the banker, Sir Charles Asgill, who was also Lord Mayor of London when the decision was taken to pull down the houses on Old London Bridge in order to improve the traffic flow. The gardens have many beautiful trees, including one of the most impressive copper beeches I have seen.

Looking downstream to your right you will see three bridges. The nearest one is a railway bridge, which was built in 1848 and was the first to take trains over the Thames in the London area. Next is Twickenham Road Bridge, constructed in 1933 of ferro-concrete with three wide spans. Beyond that is Richmond Lock and Weir together with footbridges on either side, which date from 1890. The lock and weir were designed to control the flow of the river, because after the destruction of Old London Bridge the tides

Riverside walkway in front of Richmond's
redeveloped town centre

ebbed and flowed much faster, resulting in the river here
sometimes turning into a muddy stream.

Walk upstream past Asgill House along the Thames Path
until you come to the White Cross hotel.

8. WHITE CROSS HOTEL

Note the sign by the stone steps naming them as the hotel
entrance at high tide. The towpath here is often flooded so
it can be risky to park cars here. The road leading from the
river is appropriately called Water Lane. However, the real
reason for the name is that the headquarters of the local
waterworks were situated here in the nineteenth century.

Carry on to the middle of the terrace, which slopes up from
the river to the new development overlooking the river.

9. RICHMOND BRIDGE

This five-span masonry bridge, faced with Portland stone,
was designed in 1775 by James Paine. It is the oldest

surviving river bridge in London. It was widened in 1937, but the same stone material was used to rebuild it. When you walk under the bridge you can look up and see where the new masonry joins the old. The financing of the bridge was unusual. A 'ton-tine' was set up, whereby a group of investors put up the money and took a share of the dividends which came from tolls. As each investor died, the dividends for the survivors increased until the last one finally died in 1859. After that the tolls ceased. Today the bridge leads to Twickenham, which was merged with Richmond as a London borough in 1965. The new town hall is in Twickenham across the river, but the name of the joint borough is Richmond.

The development at the top of the terrace is by the architect Quinlan Terry. It is criticised by some for being too traditional in style. However, the idea was to incorporate three of the restored old buildings into a modern development and the architect has chosen a classical style as being most sympathetic to the existing structures. Local people had objected to an earlier plan to demolish all the old buildings to create an entirely new civic centre.

The former Victorian town hall, which is set back and

The eighteenth-century Richmond Bridge –
London's oldest existing bridge structure

to the left of the development, has been turned into a community centre and houses the Richmond Museum. Inside is a large-scale model of Richmond Palace. Just to the left of the arched entrance to the central block is Heron House, which was originally built in 1690. To the far right is the nineteenth-century Tower House with its campanile.

Now walk under the bridge, not forgetting to examine the underside of the bridge arch to see where it was widened in 1937. Carry on past the landing stage, where you can take a boat to Hampton Court or back to Westminster. You will arrive at a low passage under the main road on your left. Go down the steps and emerge into Terrace Gardens.

10. TERRACE GARDENS GROTTO

In the eighteenth century the Duke of Montague owned a mansion here and constructed this passage in the form of a grotto to connect the upper part of his grounds with the lower part by the river. Today the grotto has lost most of its attractions, but at least makes it easy to cross the main road. The Duke's mansion was demolished in 1937 when the gardens were opened to the public. They are rather steep, but well worth the climb. Not far from the grotto is a statue of a river god, which came from the old mansion. As you climb you will see many fine trees, including ginkgo biloba, cedar, acer, chestnut and yew. There is a board by the greenhouse at the bottom of the gardens on the left side which identifies the main trees. When you reach the top you will find another statue, surrounded by a small pond. This is a modern statue of Aphrodite, which shows her in less flattering shape than is usual. She is known by local people as 'Bulbous Betty'.

Climb the steps to the path along Richmond Hill, turn right and walk up the hill until you reach the large display panel which describes the view from Richmond Hill.

11. RICHMOND HILL VIEWPOINT

'Heavens! What a goodly prospect spreads around, of hills and dales, and woods and lawns and spires and glittering towns and gilded streams,' exclaimed the poet James Thomson when he came to live here in 1727. Another poet to be inspired by the view and the songs of the nightingales around here was William Wordsworth, although the resulting lines were hardly his best: 'Choir of Richmond Hill, Chanting with indefatigable bill.' Among the artists who have painted this scene are Joseph Mallord William Turner and Joshua Reynolds. Further up the hill you will see Wick House, built for Reynolds by William Chambers in 1771.

Probably Richmond Hill's most important influence was on the naming of the capital of the state of Virginia. In 1737 William Byrd, a gentleman planter, looked out over the James River there and was reminded of this view. He laid out a new town by the river and named it Richmond. Look at the display panel which identifies several places which you might be able to see on a clear day if there were not so many trees in the way.

Walk on up the hill past Nightingale Lane which reminds you of Wordsworth's poem, although sadly there are no more nightingales here now. Soon after this you will pass Reynolds' home, Wick House, and then you will come to the Royal Star and Garter Home.

12. ROYAL STAR AND GARTER HOME

There used to be a grand French chateau-style hotel on this site. It went out of business and was replaced by the present home for disabled soldiers. This massive red-brick building was designed by the architect Sir Edwin Cooper in 1924, and dominates the river for miles around. The other military connection with Richmond is the British Legion poppy factory, situated below in Petersham Road. Millions of red poppies are made there every year to be sold in memory of those who died fighting for their country and to collect money to help their families.

Continue to the top of the hill and the entrance to Richmond Park.

13. RICHMOND PARK

Note the fine fountain in the wrought iron pavilion on the roundabout at the road junction. This commemorates the coronation of George VI in 1937. The park gates and lodge were designed by Sir John Soane in 1790 in the reign of George III, whose initials 'GIII R' are inscribed on them. Richmond Park used to be a royal park for hunting deer. It was opened up for public use in the 1850s and there are still over 600 deer roaming free, although it is forbidden to hunt them. Instead many recreational facilities are available, including golf courses, cricket and football pitches, a lake for fishing and over 2,000 acres of open and wooded countryside. One further reminder of its royal past remains – the name 'Henry VIII's Mound'. This is in the middle of the park at its highest point, and is supposed to be where Henry stood to await the rocket fired from the Tower of London to signal the execution of his then wife, Anne Boleyn.

The nearest railway and Underground station is Richmond, where you started. Walk back all the way down Richmond Hill and continue straight along Hill Rise, Hill Street, George Street and The Quadrant until you reach the station. This is about a 15-minute walk.

Greenwich

START: Island Gardens DLR Station. From the station, walk
    down Ferry Street towards the river and turn left onto the
    grassy area near the entrance to the Greenwich Foot Tunnel.
FINISH: Royal Naval College Chapel – the nearest station is
    Cutty Sark DLR Station.
WALKING DISTANCE: 2¼ miles
HIGHLIGHTS: *Cutty Sark*, Queen's House, Royal Observatory,
    Royal Naval College Painted Hall and Chapel.
FOOD & DRINK: The Trafalgar Inn, Royal Observatory cafeteria,
    wide variety of pubs and restaurants around the market area
    in the centre of Greenwich.

Greenwich is where time begins. Since the international conference of 1884, Greenwich Mean Time has been the standard from which all the world's times are worked out. When you reach the Royal Observatory, you can stand astride the meridian line that divides the eastern and western hemispheres. The town is steeped in maritime history. Here you will see the *Cutty Sark*, champion of the tall clippers that sailed with tea from China and wool from Australia. The Royal Naval Hospital, later the Royal Naval College, was built in the seventeenth century by several of Britain's most distinguished architects and can be visited without charge. Entry to the Queen's House, Royal Maritime Museum and Royal Observatory is also free. In fact, it is best to set aside at least a whole day to do justice to Greenwich, starting with this walk to whet your appetite.

1. ISLAND GARDENS

From your spot on the riverbank, you are looking at the famous view of Greenwich Hospital, painted by Canaletto in 1750. The painting itself is in the National Maritime Museum collection.

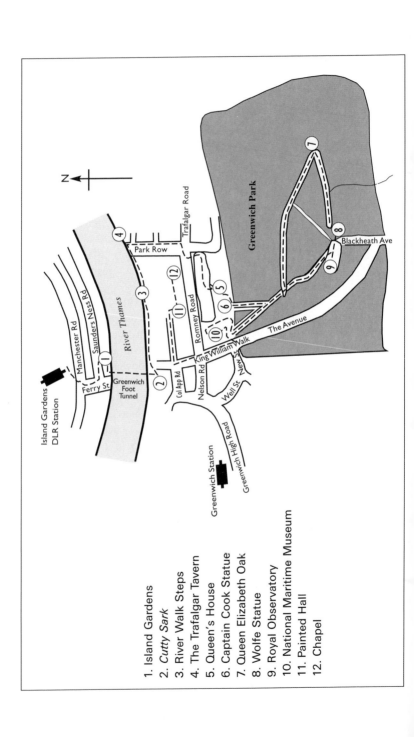

N

River Thames

Island Gardens
DLR Station

Manchester Rd
Saunders Ness Rd
Ferry St
Greenwich
Foot
Tunnel

Park Row

Trafalgar Road

Greenwich Park

Blackheath Ave

The Avenue

Col App Rd
Nelson Rd
King William Walk
Romney Road
Well St
New St

Greenwich Station

Greenwich High Road

1. Island Gardens
2. *Cutty Sark*
3. River Walk Steps
4. The Trafalgar Tavern
5. Queen's House
6. Captain Cook Statue
7. Queen Elizabeth Oak
8. Wolfe Statue
9. Royal Observatory
10. National Maritime Museum
11. Painted Hall
12. Chapel

Greenwich has been associated with the sea ever since the Viking invasions in the Dark Ages. On one incursion the invaders captured the Archbishop of Canterbury, Alfege, and murdered him. He is commemorated by St Alfege Church, built by Nicholas Hawksmoor in the baroque style, which is not far from Greenwich marketplace. Later, many monarchs, including Henry VIII and his daughter Elizabeth I, enjoyed staying here in the medieval Palace of Placentia. It was here also that the death warrants of two queens, Anne Boleyn and Mary Queen of Scots, were signed. The Palace of Placentia had fallen into disrepair by the seventeenth century, and was finally pulled down in the 1660s by Charles II. Nothing remains from the old palace, and the baroque complex you see today stands on its site.

To the right, where the river starts to curve to the north, is Deptford, which is also associated with ships and the sea. Henry VIII founded the Royal Dockyard there with a view to challenging France and Spain for naval supremacy. Many famous ships were built there including Sir Francis Drake's *Golden Hind*, the first ship to sail completely around the world.

The foot tunnel was built in 1902 to allow dockers to cross the river from Greenwich to work in the West India Docks. Previously they had to rely on a ferry. The lift was installed at the same time. Although impressive, it was not a pioneering project since Marc Brunel had already tunnelled under the Thames at Rotherhithe in 1834, and lifts were used from 1890 in the London Underground. Today's other foot tunnel under the Thames was opened in 1912 in Woolwich.

Walk back to the entrance to the foot tunnel, and go down by the stairs or lift. Walk under the river and emerge the other side by the *Cutty Sark*.

2. *CUTTY SARK*
The *Cutty Sark* was built in Scotland in 1869, made from a mixture of wood and iron. It is a wonderful sight in dry dock, but must have been inspiring in full sail on its way

to and from China. At that time, tea was brought from China to England once a year and the first ship to return obtained the highest price. The *Cutty Sark* was the fastest ship on the route and did the journey eight times, taking just under four months each way. Unfortunately the opening of the Suez Canal in the same year, 1869, put paid to the use of clippers for this trade. Steamships could use the canal to complete the voyage much more quickly than the clippers, which had to sail all the way round Africa. Consequently the *Cutty Sark* was converted for use in the Australian wool trade and was the fastest ship on this route for several years. It sailed out via the Cape of Good Hope and back via Cape Horn, averaging about 350 miles per day.

The name 'Cutty Sark' means a 'short chemise'. It is taken from the poem *Tam O'Shanter* by Robert Burns, where the hero comes upon a group of witches and is pursued by a beautiful young witch in a short chemise. He rides his horse as fast as he can and jumps across a river to safety just in time, but the witch grabs hold of the horse's tail and is left holding its hair. This is depicted in the figurehead on the prow. Inside is an exhibition of Victorian figureheads and of life for the crew of 28 aboard the tea clipper.

Nearby you will also see the much smaller *Gypsy Moth IV*. Francis Chichester was the first man to sail round the world single-handedly in this boat in 1967. He did this at the age of 66, despite having cancer. It took him 226 days, compared with the 150 days taken by the *Cutty Sark*.

Walk downstream along the riverbank past Greenwich pier, where you can take boats to London or the Thames Barrier. Continue along the Thames Path until you come to the ornamental gates fronting the central area between the two main blocks of the Royal Naval College.

3. RIVER WALK STEPS

Queen Elizabeth II knighted Francis Chichester on these steps in 1967 with the same sword used by Elizabeth I to

Former Royal Naval College viewed from the riverside steps
where Sir Francis Chichester was knighted

knight Sir Francis Drake. The steps were also used by monarchs arriving at Greenwich by river. Through the gates you can see the layout of the former Royal Naval College, with the earlier Queen's House framed in the background. The block to your front right was the first to be constructed by John Webb in the reign of Charles II. You can see the inscription 'Carolus II Rex' under the left-hand pediment. The King had intended to build a palace to rival Versailles, but the money ran out. After his death William and Mary decided to complete the complex and turn it over to be used as the Royal Naval Hospital for old or infirm sailors. The last block was not finished until the reign of Queen Anne. The hospital's regime was rather strict and it soon lost its popularity. It was transformed into the Royal Naval College in 1873. The College moved to Dartmouth at the end of the last century, and the buildings are now part of Greenwich University.

As you can see, Wren, Hawksmoor and Vanburgh, the architects of the later blocks, followed John Webb's original baroque style. The overall design, with the two domes and colonnades at the back, succeeds in foreshortening the view

The eighteenth-century warship anchor on display on the
approach to the Queen's House

of the classical Queen's House and results in a satisfying
unity despite the differing architectural styles.

Carry on along the Thames Path until you reach The Trafalgar
Tavern.

4. THE TRAFALGAR TAVERN

The tavern was built in 1837, based on the shape of
Nelson's flagship at the Battle of Trafalgar, HMS *Victory*.
With its bow windows and balconies overlooking the
Thames, it has always been a popular venue. Charles
Dickens often drank here and used it as the scene of the
wedding breakfast in *Our Mutual Friend*. In the
nineteenth century, Liberal MPs would come down by
boat from Westminster for whitebait suppers – the fish
were plentiful in the Thames estuary in those days. The
sign outside the tavern still advertises whitebait, but it is
probably not caught in the Thames today.

Walk inland up Park Row as far as the main road. Turn right and cross by the pedestrian crossing. Go into the grounds of the National Maritime Museum, walk past the display of old anchors, and continue diagonally to the right to the front of the Queen's House.

5. QUEEN'S HOUSE

This was the first classical-style building in England, commissioned by James I in 1619 for his wife, Anne of Denmark. The architect was Inigo Jones, who was influenced by Palladio, the Italian Renaissance architect. Although from the front it looks perfectly proportioned, it is in fact a most unusual building as it spans the cobbled road which today is enclosed by a colonnade. Originally this was the main road from London, and Queen Anne wanted to be able to go to the back of her house to watch the hunting in Greenwich Park without having to walk across a public road. The main road was later diverted by Charles II to where it is today. Legend has it that Sir Walter Raleigh laid his cloak out on the old road to allow Elizabeth I to cross it without muddying her feet.

Entry to the house is free, so you should at least go

A cobbled street under the Queen's House where Queen Elizabeth I is said to have walked over Sir Walter Raleigh's cloak to avoid a puddle

111

inside to see the Great Hall, which is a 40-foot cube structure, designed by Inigo Jones in accordance with Palladio's rules of classical proportion. You can also admire the magnificent black and white chequered marble floor and the round Tulip Stairs, so-called because of the tulip motifs in the wrought iron balustrade. The ceiling painting by Orazio and Artemisia Gentileschi was removed to Marlborough House in the eighteenth century as a favour from Queen Anne to her friend Sarah, Duchess of Marlborough. The Queen must have regretted this later when they fell out. Until 2003 there was a laser reproduction here, but this has now also disappeared.

Come out of the Great Hall on to the cobbled walkway which used to be the main road. Walk to the right along the colonnade and then turn left towards the park. Just to the right is a statue to Captain James Cook.

6. CAPTAIN COOK STATUE

This statue of the famous eighteenth-century navigator, Captain James Cook, was carved in 1997. He is looking up to the top of the hill where you will see a statue of General James Wolfe, the captor of Quebec. They went on a voyage together to chart the St Lawrence River in Canada. Their map is still accepted as accurate.

From here there is a good view of the Royal Observatory, designed by Sir Christopher Wren in the Dutch style. It is the red-brick building with white quoins and a red ball on top. The red ball ascends to the top of the pole at 12.55 p.m. each day, and descends at exactly 1 p.m. This was done so that sailors in the past could set their clocks to Greenwich Mean Time, and the tradition is still maintained today. Wren was given a strict budget of £500 for the construction of the Observatory. He had to save costs by painting in the two side windows, which look like real windows, and by making the quoins of painted wood rather than expensive Portland stone. He still went over budget by £20 9s 1d in old currency.

Walk along the path to the right, enter the park and follow the path towards the Observatory. Take the second branch left, just before the steep ascent to the Observatory. Carry on until you are nearly directly in line with Wolfe's statue. Here you will find the dead stump of an oak tree behind some railings.

7. QUEEN ELIZABETH OAK

The original oak tree was planted in the 1200s. It died in the nineteenth century but remained standing until it finally collapsed in 1991. Elizabeth I is supposed to have sat under this tree when she signed the order to attack the Spanish Armada in 1588. She must have had mixed feelings about coming to Greenwich because it was also here that her father, Henry VIII, signed the death warrant of her mother, Anne Boleyn. The Duke of Edinburgh planted the new oak tree that you see beside the collapsed Queen Elizabeth Oak in 1992. Hopefully this tree will also live for several centuries.

Turn right and climb up to the top of the hill.

8. WOLFE STATUE

Like Lord Nelson, James Wolfe was a commander who led from the front. He died in 1759 at the moment of his greatest triumph after his assault on Quebec and is buried in the Church of St Alfege in Greenwich. His statue, sculpted in 1930 by Tait Mackenzie, looks out over a panorama of the river, with London in the distance. To the right you see the ill-starred but imposing Millennium Dome, designed by Richard Rogers. It was constructed at a cost of £750 million to celebrate the Millennium, but only achieved half its visitor target and the Government was left to foot the bill. Its future remains uncertain at the time of writing. It is possible to walk there along the riverside, but you should allow 45 minutes. Alternatively you can reach it via the Jubilee Line to North Greenwich Station.

Below is the Queen's House, Royal Maritime Museum and Royal Naval College, with a view of the towering Canary Wharf development through the middle. To the left you can see the *Cutty Sark* and also, on a clear day, famous London sights such as Tower Bridge and St Paul's Cathedral.

Now enter the courtyard by the Royal Observatory and stand astride the meridian line.

9. ROYAL OBSERVATORY

The meridian line divides the eastern from the western hemisphere and is the place where the world's time has been measured since the International Time Conference of 1884. The red ball drops daily from the pole above Wren's Observatory building at exactly 1 p.m. You might think this would always use Greenwich Mean Time, but in fact in the summer it uses British Summer Time which is one hour later. The exact time is shown by the Accurist clock on the meridian line. The figures at the top of the clock face show the number of days since the beginning of the third millennium.

Wren's building is known as Flamsteed House, after the first Astronomer Royal, John Flamsteed. His successor, Edmond Halley (of Halley's Comet fame) also used this building, but later Astronomers Royal added further buildings, including the Meridian Building from where the meridian line starts, and the Onion Dome which contains the largest refracting telescope in Britain. Today the Royal Observatory has been moved to Cambridge because the night skies are much clearer away from the lights of London.

Walk to the far corner of the courtyard and go into the walkway at the front of Flamsteed House to see how Wren painted in the two side windows on the first floor. You can go inside to see where Flamsteed and his successors worked. There is also an exhibition of astronomical instruments and clocks. This tells the story of John Harrison's efforts to invent a precision timepiece which finally allowed ships to establish their longitudinal position. Entry is free, but be aware that you need at least an hour to appreciate what you will see here.

Now walk down the steep path immediately in front of the Observatory and carry on straight down to the National Maritime Museum. To reach the entrance you have to walk to the right to the colonnade and then go round to the other side of the building. This is well signposted.

10. NATIONAL MARITIME MUSEUM

This building with its colonnade dates from 1807 when it was used for dormitories, schoolrooms and a gymnasium. Since 1937 it has been taken over by the National Maritime Museum. It is not possible to describe here the rich contents of this museum, which covers the whole history of man's association with the sea. As well as traditional displays of maritime paintings and ships from all ages, there is modern technology that allows you to take the helm of a Viking ship or a paddle steamer. One section especially relevant to Greenwich is devoted to Lord Nelson and the Battle of Trafalgar, where you can see the uniform he wore when he was killed in 1805, with the hole through which the lethal musket ball passed.

Exit the museum back into the park and turn right to go out of the park down King William Walk on your right. Carry on down this road until you reach Romney Road, which you can cross using the pedestrian crossing. The entrance to the Royal Naval College buildings is a little further down King William Walk on your right opposite College Approach Road. Go in through the gates and continue for about 150 metres to the first of the two large domed buildings.

11. PAINTED HALL

This was the dining hall of the Royal Naval Hospital when it was built in the reign of William and Mary according to the overall design of Sir Christopher Wren. It is housed in the domed King William block and stands opposite the matching Queen Mary block which houses the Chapel. Here you can admire close-up the symmetry of Wren's design as the colonnades with their coupled Doric columns lead your eyes from the baroque domes at the front to the purely classical Queen's House at the back.

Go inside to see the hall which has been painted all over by James Thornhill in the baroque manner. The scenes are allegorical, praising the rule of William and Mary and their Hanoverian successors. It was here that Lord Nelson lay in state after his death at the Battle of Trafalgar in 1805. His body had been laid in a wooden coffin filled with brandy to preserve it on its journey back to England. It is said that, on arrival, the sailors who were bearing the coffin drank the brandy when transferring the body to the funeral coffin.

You can now visit the Chapel which is on the opposite side of the open space leading up to the Queen's House.

12. CHAPEL

The interior provides a fine contrast with the flamboyant Baroque paintings of Thornhill. It was redecorated after a fire in 1779 by James 'Athenian' Stuart in the neo-classical style, using intricate patterns of plaster mouldings on pale-blue Wedgwood coloured backgrounds. Above the altar is a painting by the American artist, Benjamin West, the second president of the Royal Academy. It depicts the rescue of St Paul after his ship was wrecked at Malta. According to the Bible, he was bitten by a viper and the local inhabitants were so amazed that he survived that they believed he must have come from God and were converted on the spot. The maritime adventure seems an appropriate theme for this Chapel.

After visiting the chapel you could walk towards the river, past the statue of George II. Just before you reach the gates where the Queen knighted Sir Francis Chichester you will see an inscription marking the site of the great Tudor palace and recording the fact that Henry VIII and his two daughters were born here.

For refreshments, there are many pubs, restaurants and snack bars in the centre of Greenwich, on the other side of King William Walk. To return to London you have three main possibilities: for mainline trains to London Bridge you can walk from the town centre about 500 metres along Greenwich High Road to Greenwich Station; the nearest Docklands Light Railway station is Cutty Sark for Maritime Greenwich, which is only 100 metres to the south-west of the *Cutty Sark* itself; finally, you may like to catch a boat back to London – several companies offer a variety of services from Greenwich Pier near the foot tunnel exit.

CHAPTER 3

Docklands Walks

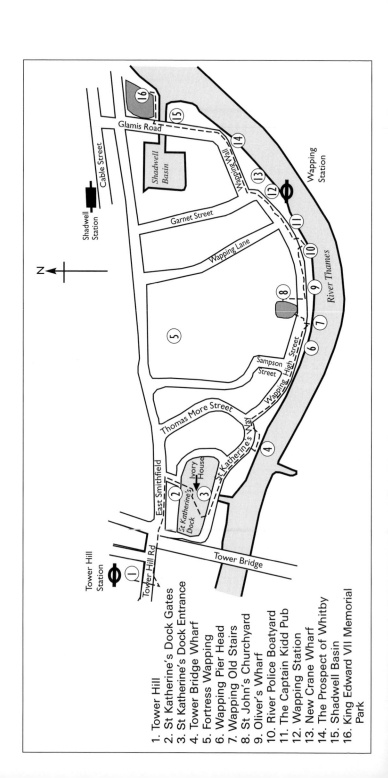

1. Tower Hill
2. St Katherine's Dock Gates
3. St Katherine's Dock Entrance
4. Tower Bridge Wharf
5. Fortress Wapping
6. Wapping Pier Head
7. Wapping Old Stairs
8. St John's Churchyard
9. Oliver's Wharf
10. River Police Boatyard
11. The Captain Kidd Pub
12. Wapping Station
13. New Crane Wharf
14. The Prospect of Whitby
15. Shadwell Basin
16. King Edward VII Memorial Park

Wapping and the London Docks

START: Tower Hill Underground Station.
FINISH: King Edward VII Memorial Park – the nearest station is
    Wapping or Shadwell.
WALKING DISTANCE: 2 miles
HIGHLIGHTS: St Katherine's Dock, Wapping Old Stairs, The
    Prospect of Whitby.
FOOD & DRINK: The Dickens Inn, The Town of Ramsgate, The
    Captain Kidd and The Prospect of Whitby pubs.

The most famous building in Wapping is a pub, The
Prospect of Whitby, which was a favourite with pirates
and smugglers as well as with Charles Dickens and
Samuel Pepys. This ancient village which stretches
between the Tower of London and Limehouse has always
been associated with seafarers. They tended to live a life
apart from the rest of London, although in the eighteenth
century the 36 pubs along the riverfront attracted many
visitors including Dr Samuel Johnson. Three of these
pubs survive. The London Docks were built in the early
nineteenth century and were famous for the import of
rum, wine and tobacco. The docks were closed in 1969,
but many of the former wharves and warehouses have
been preserved and converted into modern apartments.
This retains the atmosphere of the past although the sense
of danger evoked by Charles Dickens's novels has
vanished. The walk starts and ends with two attractive
conversions of old docks into modern usage – St
Katherine's Dock and Shadwell Basin.

1. TOWER HILL
Go up to the viewing platform. Beyond the Tower of
London is the stretch of river between Tower Bridge and
London Bridge known as the Pool of London. Until the

nineteenth century this was where ships from all over the world unloaded their cargoes. The resultant congestion and pilfering from ships waiting to land caused the Government to instigate the construction of inland dock basins surrounded by walls to the east of the Tower. All the docks were built through private finance with incentives such as 21-year trade monopolies. For various reasons the dock companies were not profitable and in 1909 the Port of London Authority (PLA) was set up to control all docks in the London area. The tall white building in the Edwardian baroque style to your right was the headquarters of the PLA until 1971 when the docks were in the process of being closed down. Today all cargo is handled at the Container Port at Tilbury in the Thames Estuary while London Docklands has been redeveloped.

Go down the steps and through the underpass under Tower Hill Road. On the other side ascend the steps to Tower Hill Road and walk along to East Smithfield, crossing Tower Bridge Approach via the pedestrian crossing. Continue along East Smithfield until you reach the entrance gates to St Katherine's Dock on your right.

2. ST KATHERINE'S DOCK GATES

The gates have one elephant on either side, reminding you that this was once the centre of the ivory trade in London. The demand for ivory was very high as every lady was expected to play the piano in Victorian times. In the centre of the dock you can see the Ivory House with a weather vane on top. This is the only original warehouse left, now converted for leisure use.

Thomas Telford constructed the dock in 1828. The name St Katherine's comes from the twelfth-century religious foundation, which has always been under the patronage of the reigning queen. It provided refuge for a community of poor people. The foundation still exists and has been relocated to Limehouse.

The aim of this dock was to take business from the earlier docks that were constructed to the east, further

Elephant on top of the entrance gates to St Katherine's Dock

from the City of London. Unfortunately the railways were invented soon afterwards, and so it was more convenient to unload cargoes with rail access further downstream than for the ships to come all the way up to the Tower Bridge area. The enterprise was not successful and was soon taken over by the London Dock Company. St Katherine's was the first to close after the collapse of the docks in the 1970s, and the first to be converted to modern use – in this case a marina.

Walk straight ahead with the western dock basin on your right. When you reach the end of the Ivory House, turn right and walk round the dock basin until you reach the bridge over the dock entrance.

3. ST KATHERINE'S DOCK ENTRANCE
The lock gates by the river control the water levels so that ships can enter and leave the dock. Except at high tide, the water level of the dock is considerably higher than that of the Thames. In fact the difference in the level of the Thames between high and low tide is over six metres. The fine yellow-brick house just by the river on the other side

of the lock gates is the original dockmaster's house, designed by the architect Philip Hardwick, who also designed Euston Station.

One of the most interesting of the impressive boats often moored here is the *Grand Turk*, which is a modern reconstruction of an eighteenth-century warship. As well as modern luxury yachts, you can see several traditional Thames sailing barges with their brown sails. These used to sail up the Thames with cargoes of hay and other goods, and could be controlled by a man and a boy. Several have now been converted for leisure use. They still occasionally sail the Thames and are a magnificent sight on a sunny day.

To the east of the dock basin is The Dickens Inn. This was opened in 1976 by Charles Dickens's great-grandson, but otherwise has nothing to do with the author himself. The timber frame from an old eighteenth-century brewery was used in its construction.

Carry on across the bridge and exit the dock into St Katherine's Way. In about 300 metres you will come to a path on your right which leads to the river.

4. TOWER BRIDGE WHARF

Here you have fine views of Tower Bridge from the less familiar eastern side, as well as Shad Thames on the South Bank. You can identify, from right to left, The Anchor Brewhouse, Butler's Wharf, the Design Museum, St Saviours Dock and China Wharf, as described in the Pool of London and Shad Thames walk in Chapter 1.

Go to the end of the river walkway and return to St Katherine's Way. Continue into Wapping High Street until you see a large grey concrete structure at a distance of about 300 metres through gaps in the houses on the left side of the road.

5. FORTRESS WAPPING

This is the printing works of Rupert Murdoch's News International Group, which publishes *The Times* and *The Sun* as well as many other titles. It was the first of the newspaper groups to desert Fleet Street for the cheaper Docklands location in 1986. The name 'Fortress Wapping' is appropriate for the rather forbidding building, but actually comes from the fierce demonstrations by the printing unions who besieged the works to try and prevent the use of new technology which would result in a considerable loss of traditional jobs.

Continue along Wapping High Street until you come to Wapping Pier Head.

6. WAPPING PIER HEAD

This was the entrance to the London Docks, designed by John Rennie in 1805. The docks were given a 21-year monopoly of all imports of tobacco, rice, wine and brandy, except those from the East and West Indies. Daniel Alexander built the yellow-brick houses on either side of the entrance in 1813 for dock officials. They were converted into luxury homes in the 1970s after the closure of the London Docks in 1969. The dock entrance and two of the three dock basins were covered over during redevelopment in the 1970s.

Just up Wapping High Street you can see the pub sign of The Town of Ramsgate, showing a picture of Ramsgate harbour in the nineteenth century. The pub is named after the fishermen from Ramsgate who came to sell fish at Wapping Old Stairs.

When you come to The Town of Ramsgate, walk to the right down the narrow passage to the river.

7. WAPPING OLD STAIRS

If the tide is out you can descend the steps onto the riverbed, but be careful as it is slippery. These stairs have

An unusual view of Tower Bridge, from
the riverbed at Wapping Old Stairs

a gruesome history. Pirates were hanged nearby in
Execution Dock and their corpses brought here so that
they were washed over by the tide three times. This
caused them to be swollen and people said 'What a
whopper!' – hence the name Wapping. It was also here
that the notorious Judge Jeffreys was apprehended in
1689 when trying to escape to France disguised as a
sailor. He was taken to the Tower, but died before he
could be executed.

Return to Wapping High Street and cross over into the
churchyard.

8. ST JOHN'S CHURCHYARD

This was the churchyard of St John's, Wapping. The
church itself was built in 1756 in red brick with white
stone dressings, so that it would stand out amidst the dark
and murky atmosphere of the area. It was bombed in the
Second World War and only the tower remains. The
building was converted into apartments after the removal
of over 100 bodies from the crypt. Next door is the former

Charity School with the figure of a boy over one entrance and a girl over the other.

Return to Wapping High Street and cross to the opposite side of the road.

9. OLIVER'S WHARF

This is a good example of an 1870s warehouse that has been converted into apartments. Next to it is Orient Wharf, a modern development with red cranes that fits in well with the older buildings. It comprises shared-ownership flats for local residents. The redevelopment of Docklands has had a marked effect on the pattern of home ownership in the area. Before the 1970s council tenants occupied over 90 per cent of the houses, whereas today about half the properties are privately owned.

Walk a little further and turn right onto the riverside.

10. RIVER POLICE BOATYARD

The Thames River Police was established in 1797 and was the first uniformed police force in the world. At the time crime was a major problem on the river and was one of the reasons for building the inland docks enclosed by high walls. Today the main problems are stolen yachts and attempted suicides. The blue and white building houses the police boats and provides maintenance facilities. The present headquarters is just up the road and houses a museum (visits by appointment only).

The open area by the river was known as Execution Dock and is where many pirates were executed up to 1814. Look across the river to Rotherhithe and you can identify several buildings, including The Angel pub and St Mary's Church, described in the Rotherhithe and the Surrey Docks walk on page 133. Canary Wharf is in the distance to your left.

Continue along Wapping High Street to The Captain Kidd pub.

11. THE CAPTAIN KIDD PUB

The second of the historic riverside pubs commemorates the famous pirate, Captain Kidd. He was in fact a wealthy man, having married an heiress, and so did not need to resort to piracy. He was finally caught and executed in 1701. Go into the pub where a board on the right of the entrance passage records his story. There is also a gibbet in the pub's riverside garden.

Carry on to Wapping Station.

12. WAPPING STATION

This is the North Bank entrance to Brunel's famous tunnel described in the Rotherhithe and the Surrey Docks walk. If you have an appropriate Zone 2 travelcard you can descend the original shaft onto the platform of what is today Wapping East London Line Station. Here you can see fascinating historical pictures of the tunnel starting from its original use as a foot tunnel.

Continue along to the end of Wapping High Street.

13. NEW CRANE WHARF

Originally constructed in 1873, this is one of the most spectacular warehouse conversions in Wapping. You see three Victorian warehouses surrounding a cobbled yard with red cranes to add to the atmosphere of the old docks. The buildings are still marked with the letters H, G and F, which identified the different warehouses. Today, expensive apartments, shops and restaurants occupy the space. The cookery author and television presenter, Delia Smith, owns one of the apartments here.

Now turn to the right off Wapping High Street into Wapping Wall and carry on to the end of this road.

The Thames Path at Blackfriars, looking from under
the railway bridge to the road bridge, opened by
Queen Victoria in 1869

Middle Temple
Hall with the
rose garden
where the
Wars of the
Roses started,
according to
William
Shakespeare

The view from
Westminster
Bridge that
Wordsworth
never saw

An alleyway behind
The Dove,
Hammersmith's
oldest riverside pub

Kew Gardens' wrought-iron entrance gates,
constructed in 1848

The view from Richmond Hill which inspired poets,
painters and a Virginian planter

Canaletto's painting of this view of Greenwich from Island Gardens can be seen in Queen's House

The *Cutty Sark* with the carved prow depicting the witch holding Tam O'Shanter's horse's tail

Luxury yachts moored in front of Ivory House, where cargo ships used to unload

The Mayflower pub near St Mary's Church where the ship's owner, Captain Jones, is buried

Dramatic architecture at the Isle of Dogs Storm
Water Pumping Station

The vast expanse of the Royal Victoria Dock Basin

Glaxo SmithKline's modern glass head office has replaced older industries on the canal bank

A vibrant-looking Chinese restaurant by the Cumberland Basin

The Viaduct near one of the many
sources of the River Fleet

The view from Blackfriars Station of the now
demolished London, Dover and Chatham Railway
Bridge. Behind is Blackfriars Road Bridge, under
which flows the River Fleet

14. THE PROSPECT OF WHITBY

This claims to be the oldest riverside pub in London. It was first built in 1520 and preserves much of its original interior but the outside was rebuilt in the nineteenth century. You can see a list of all the monarchs who have been on the throne throughout the life of the pub, starting with Henry VIII. The pub's original name was The Devil's Tavern as it was associated with thieves and smugglers. In the riverside beer garden is a gibbet to remind you of this history. The name was changed in the eighteenth century because a collier ship called the *Prospect* brought coal from Whitby in Yorkshire to the hydraulic pumping station which is to the north of the pub.

Walk on to the red bascule bridge.

The Prospect of Whitby and a gibbet,
viewed from the riverbed

15. SHADWELL BASIN

This bridge was built in the 1930s over the entrance to Shadwell Basin. It was originally controlled by hydraulic power from the tall red-brick pumping station on the south-east corner of the dock basin. Power from here was also piped to the centre of London to raise theatre curtains in Leicester Square. This was probably the last operating hydraulic pumping station in the world and only closed down in 1977. Today it contains a café and is used for theatrical performances and exhibitions.

Shadwell Basin itself is the only remaining basin of the London Docks. Colourful housing surrounds it. Houses are privately owned, but a special 33 per cent discount allows teachers to live near their inner-city schools. Cormorants often sit on the raft in the middle of the water waiting to catch various fish such as carp, bream and roach. On the river side of the bridge is a watersports training centre for local children. You now have a much closer view of Canary Wharf.

Walk over the bridge, then turn right off Glamis Road into the pathway, keeping the watersports centre on your right. When you reach the river, turn left and walk behind the round red-brick structure with the glass-domed roof.

16. KING EDWARD VII MEMORIAL PARK

The park was opened as a recreation area for local people in 1922 after the death of King Edward VII. By the round building you can see a plaque commemorating famous sixteenth-century navigators. Willoughby, for example, set out with a small fleet to discover a north-east passage to Asia but perished when his ship became icebound in the Arctic. One ship in his fleet did get through to Russia where the crew were greeted by the Russian Tsar, Ivan the Terrible. The building itself is the North Bank ventilation shaft for the Rotherhithe Road Tunnel which was constructed in 1908 as a twin bore road tunnel. From the riverside you can see the South Bank ventilation shaft just to the right of the red bridge at the entrance to the former Surrey Commercial Docks.

The walk ends here. The nearest stations are Wapping on the East London Line, which you passed on your way, or Shadwell on the Docklands Light Railway (DLR), which you can reach by returning to Glamis Road and then turning right. Carry on as far as Cable Street, turn left and you will find the station in about 400 metres on the right of the road. This should take no more than ten minutes.

For a longer but more attractive route, you can continue along the Thames path to Limehouse and follow the signs to Limehouse DLR Station. This will take about 20 minutes at a medium pace.

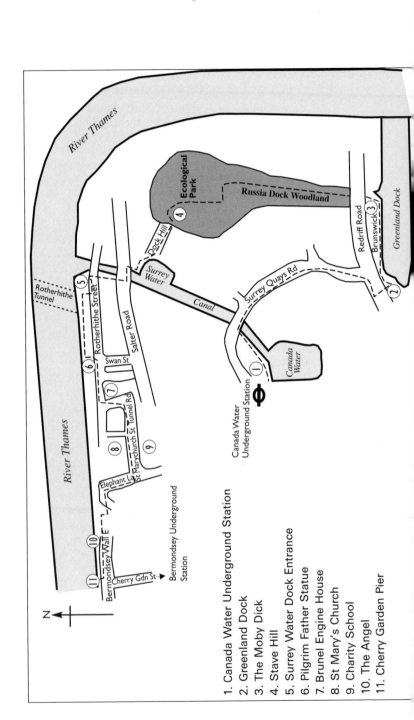

1. Canada Water Underground Station
2. Greenland Dock
3. The Moby Dick
4. Stave Hill
5. Surrey Water Dock Entrance
6. Pilgrim Father Statue
7. Brunel Engine House
8. St Mary's Church
9. Charity School
10. The Angel
11. Cherry Garden Pier

Rotherhithe and the Surrey Docks

START: Canada Water Underground Station (Lower Road exit).

FINISH: Cherry Garden Pier, Rotherhithe – the nearest Underground is Bermondsey.

WALKING DISTANCE: 2¾ miles

HIGHLIGHTS: Greenland Dock, Brunel Engine House, St Mary's Church.

FOOD & DRINK: The Moby Dick, The Mayflower and The Angel pubs.

This whole area was covered by the dock basins and warehouses of the former Surrey Docks until the 1970s. Most have now been filled in and converted into housing, industrial buildings or landscaped parkland. The remaining areas of water provide an attractive setting for the new developments as well as a reminder of the history of the docks. After walking past two of the old dock basins and through a new woodland you come to the village of Rotherhithe. This has always been associated with seafarers and nautical trades, and today still retains its village atmosphere. Two important events started here – the setting out of the *Mayflower* to America in 1620, and the building of the Thames Tunnel by Marc and Isambard Kingdom Brunel in 1834. You will see the Brunel Engine House, The Mayflower pub and St Mary's Church where Christopher Jones, captain of the *Mayflower*, is buried.

1. CANADA WATER UNDERGROUND STATION

Canada Water Underground Station, from which you have just emerged, is one of the most exciting new stations built for the Jubilee Line Extension in 1999. It has been likened to an underground St Paul's Cathedral. This was the largest engineering project in Europe at the time, resulting in the building of 12 new stations and tunnelling under three stretches of the Thames. It provides much-needed access to public transport for this area and East London in general.

The name of the station recalls the old Canada Dock – a vast area of water surrounded by wharves and warehouses. Today you see the small stretch of water called Canada Pond in front of the 1988 shopping centre development. At a distance of about 50 metres on the right-hand side of Canada Pond you will see a statue of a deal porter. Deal porters were dockers who carried incredibly large loads of wooden planks balanced on their heads by the use of special hats. Timber was the main cargo in Canada Dock.

Walk along the left side of Canada Water by the canal until you come to steps leading up to Surrey Quays Road. Ascend the steps and go to the right past the Harmsworth Press building. The *Daily Mail* and *Evening Standard* newspapers are printed here. When you come to the end of Surrey Quays Road, turn right into Redriff Road. Shortly you will see a large red bridge on the other side of the road. Cross over and descend the steps to the paved area by the waterside.

2. GREENLAND DOCK

The first large inland wet dock in London was built here in 1700. It was called the Howland Dock, and could accommodate up to 120 ships. It was about half the length of the present dock and was lined with trees to give protection from the stormy winds which caused havoc among the ships moored on the congested Thames. In 1763 it was leased to the South Sea Company for its whaling fleet and renamed Greenland Dock.

In the second half of the nineteenth century, all the docks in the area were amalgamated into the Surrey Commercial Docks Company, which enlarged the Greenland Dock to this point so as to connect it up with Canada Dock. The engineer responsible was John Wolfe-Barry who, together with Horace Jones, also designed

Tower Bridge. The connecting channel, which used to be at the end of the dock by Redriff Road, was closed in when the area was redeveloped in the 1970s.

Walk along Brunswick Quay on the left side of the dock until you come to the inlet.

3. THE MOBY DICK

In the 1800s whales from the arctic were boiled here in large 'coppers' to make oil for lighting the streets of London. They also made a foul stench, well described in Melville's *Moby Dick* as being like excavating an old city graveyard. The Moby Dick pub on the opposite side of the inlet reminds you of all this whaling activity. Today the Greenland Dock is the largest of the three remaining dock basins out of the original eleven owned by the Surrey Commercial Docks Company. It is now surrounded mainly by private houses and sailing clubs.

You can see the capstan and jigger used to open the lock gates, which have now been closed in. These led to the beginning of the ill-starred Grand Surrey Canal, which was originally planned to run as far as Portsmouth, but never in fact went further than Peckham. Instead, the excavated canal was expanded to form the Norway and Russia Docks which have now been turned into a nature park. The channel linking the Greenland and Norway Docks has been bounded by walls on which you can see the depth of the water marked on the far side of the road tunnel. The deepest mark is 21 feet.

Go under the road bridge into the Russia Dock Woodland. This is a pleasant area of natural countryside with a stream running through the middle. Follow the path straight along until you come to the sign for Stave Hill. Turn left and follow further signs for Stave Hill. When you come to a tall round mound, go up the steps which are on the far side. The distance from Greenland Dock is about half a mile.

4. STAVE HILL

The name comes from the small Stave Dock which led into Russia Dock. Here you have a view over the Surrey Docks area, and also of more distant sights such as Canary Wharf. Examine the circular bronze model which shows the layout of the former Surrey Docks. If it has rained recently, the dock basins and canals in the model will be filled with water, giving a realistic impression of the area before the docks were filled in during the 1970s.

You can orientate yourself to the map by identifying the gas works, which are on the bottom right side of the map as you look at it after coming up the steps. Look behind you and you will see the only remaining gas-holder of the South Metropolitan Gas Company works which fronted the Thames so that sea coal could easily be landed. Gas production ceased in 1959. Looking further round to your right you can see the Harmworth Printing Works, behind which is Canada Water, where you started. In front of you is the nature park, which was mainly dock basins, as you see from the map. Stave Hill is shown in the centre of the map and is located in the former Russia Dock.

Descend the steps and walk straight along Dock Hill until you reach the third remaining dock, known as Surrey Water. As you go round the right side of the dock, look at the amusing modern bronze statue of three woodland figures in red shoes on the grassy area. Then continue until the main road, where you must mount the steps to cross it and then continue until you reach the riverside.

5. SURREY WATER DOCK ENTRANCE

This was the northern entrance to the Surrey Docks from the Thames. The red bascule bridge would originally have been raised by hydraulic power. Beatson's ship-breaking yard operated near where The Spice Island pub now is to your right. It was famous for breaking the *Temeraire* in 1838. This ship, which had fought at the Battle of Trafalgar, was immortalised by J.M.W. Turner in his romantic painting *The Fighting Temeraire*, now in the National Gallery.

Red Bridge at the northern entrance to the old Surrey Docks

To the western side of the dock entrance is a round red-brick structure. This is one of two ventilation shafts for the Rotherhithe Road Tunnel, built in 1908. You can see a similar structure on the other side of the river to the north-east. These shafts are placed near the river because the approach roads descend below the ground as far from the riverbanks as the river is wide. Immediately opposite on the other side of the river is the oldest pub in London – The Prospect of Whitby.

From the riverbank, walk back to Rotherhithe Street and turn right past the back of the ventilation shaft. Turn right immediately onto the riverside path and continue along this until the path ends, where you will see the Pilgrim Father statue.

6. PILGRIM FATHER STATUE

This statue commemorates the sailing of the *Mayflower* from Rotherhithe to America with the Pilgrim Fathers in 1620. It is a charming fantasy, showing a modern young boy reading the *Sunbeam Weekly* comic, with the spirit of a Pilgrim Father standing behind him and casting the

Statue of a Pilgrim Father casting the shadow of the story of the *Mayflower* onto a boy's comic

shadow of the story of the *Mayflower* onto its pages. As well as depicting the *Mayflower* and its epic voyage, the sculptor has brought the story up to date by showing images of the USA today.

You now have to turn inland back to Rotherhithe Street where you turn right and shortly will arrive at the Brunel Engine House.

7. BRUNEL ENGINE HOUSE

This is the original pump house used during the construction of the Thames Tunnel between 1824 and 1843. It was the first tunnel built under a major river since Roman times. After two previous attempts had failed, Marc Brunel undertook the project using his invention of a tunnelling shield which allowed the workers to bore manually into the subsoil and line the walls of the resulting tunnel shaft as the work progressed. This method is still used today, except that manual labour has been replaced by machines. It was dangerous work and ten people died in the construction of the tunnel. Marc Brunel himself was injured and his son, Isambard Kingdom Brunel, nearly drowned when the partially completed tunnel was flooded.

The tunnel was opened in 1843 by Queen Victoria to great acclaim but the money had run out before the planned ramps, which would have allowed horse-drawn carriages to use the tunnel, were built. It was used as a foot tunnel until in 1869 the East London Line took it over to transport passengers by rail under the river between Rotherhithe and Wapping. Today the service has been extended as far south as New Cross.

Walk inland past the Brunel Engine House and turn right into Tunnel Road. Note the former nineteenth-century warehouses which have been converted to modern use. The one on the corner just before you reach St Mary's church is now Sands Film Studios. Towards the river you will see other converted warehouses as well as The Mayflower pub with its ship weathervane. Shortly you will come to St Marychurch Street.

8. ST MARY'S CHURCH

The church was built in 1715 to a design by John James, the architect of St George's Church in Hanover Square. A petition to Parliament that a new parish church should be built was turned down, so local people raised £4,000 and did much of the work themselves. It is a red-brick building with stone dressings. The tower has louvred belfry openings with clock faces below and a balustrade above, crowned by a short spire.

Christopher Jones, who captained the *Mayflower* on the voyage to America in 1620, was buried here in 1622. There is a modern memorial to him in the churchyard to the west of the church. Just behind this statue is the tomb of Prince Lee Boo, the son of the King of the Pelau Islands. A local man, Captain Wilson, was sailing in the South Pacific when his ship was wrecked there in 1735 and he received such kindness from the King that he agreed to bring his son back to Rotherhithe to further his education. Sadly, the prince died soon after from smallpox.

You can normally enter the church at the back of the nave, although the nave itself is closed. Looking through the screen you can see many features related to the seafaring occupations of the parishioners. The four Ionic columns seem to be made of stone, but in fact are ship's masts made from tree trunks, encased in plaster. The roof looks like an upturned boat. The two bishop's chairs are made from oak wood that was once part of the ship *Temeraire*, painted by Turner.

After visiting the church, cross the road to the former Charity School building.

9. CHARITY SCHOOL

Charity Schools were common in England from the seventeenth century. Typically, they had the statue of a boy and girl above the entrance, as is the case here. It is recorded that Prince Lee Boo studied here. The school moved to larger premises in 1900. Next to the school building is an open area that used to be the overflow graveyard. According to the sign on the corner, there was a watchhouse here to deter body-snatchers from stealing corpses to sell to hospitals for experimental dissection.

On the other side of the road is Hope Sufferance Wharf. In Tudor times the so-called 'Legal Quays' were set up near London Bridge so that customs duties could be collected. Soon the river by London Bridge became so congested that 'Sufferance Wharves' were allowed further downstream for storage of lower-duty cargoes. The building is currently in the process of being converted.

Carry on along St Marychurch Street and then turn right into Elephant Lane. Turn right off this road where it bends back inland. Go along the riverside path until you come to The Angel pub.

10. THE ANGEL

It is recorded that the monks of nearby Bermondsey Abbey kept an inn here in the fifteenth century. Samuel Pepys stayed in a later inn when he visited the nearby chalybeate springs in the seventeenth century. The present nineteenth-century building is one of the few remaining galleried inns in London and has an upstairs restaurant with fine views of the river.

On the riverside terrace just past the pub you will find three bronze statues. The man sitting on the bench is Dr Salter, a popular local MP from early in the twentieth century. His daughter, who sadly died young, is standing by the river wall and next to her, lurking on the river wall, is her cat.

The grassy mound with ruined walls is all that remains from the fourteenth-century manor house of Edward III, only recently rediscovered in 1980. Three panels tell of its history.

Carry on along the path until you reach some steps which lead up to a terrace right by the river.

Dr Salter's daughter's cat on the river wall at Cherry Garden Pier

141

11. CHERRY GARDEN PIER

This was where Samuel Pepys visited the chalybeate springs and cherry garden as described in his diaries. It was also the place from which J.M.W. Turner painted *The Fighting Temeraire*. You can enjoy the views upstream of Tower Bridge and, beyond that, of the City of London. Across the river is the white and blue structure of the Thames River Police boathouse.

If you decide to take refreshments now, you can retrace your steps to The Angel or The Mayflower pubs. The nearest Underground station is Bermondsey. Walk inland to the end of Cherry Garden Street and turn right along the main road until you come to the pedestrian crossing opposite the station.

Canary Wharf and
the West India Docks

START: Westferry DLR Station. Walk down the steps from Westferry DLR Station, cross Westferry Road and continue along the right side of the railway until you reach Garford Street. There are some cottages here, built in 1807 for the West India Dock Police. When you reach Garford Street turn left under the railway, and then immediately right. A few metres further on the right is an Indian restaurant.

FINISH: South Quay DLR Station.

WALKING DISTANCE: 3 miles

HIGHLIGHTS: West India Quay warehouses, Museum in Docklands, Storm Water Pumping Station, Blue Bridge, No. 1 Canada Square, Canary Wharf Jubilee Line Station.

FOOD & DRINK: Canary Wharf has a wide variety of waterside restaurants, bars and pubs.

The area known as the Isle of Dogs is actually a peninsula stretching from Aspen Way in the north to Island Gardens in the south. It was mainly desolate marshland until the West India Docks were built in 1802. They were the first of the many inland dock basins to be excavated and they roughly cover the location of this walk. First, you will pass some of the nineteenth-century houses where dock officials lived, and then you enter the former dock gates beside which are some magnificent Grade I listed warehouses. These have been converted for residential and leisure use and today house the Museum in Docklands. The walk then takes you around the modern Canary Wharf development where there is a wide variety of architectural styles, street sculpture and landscaping. You will also find many reminders of the former docks, such as bridges, cranes and the remains of the dock basins themselves. Finally, you will have a chance to see the

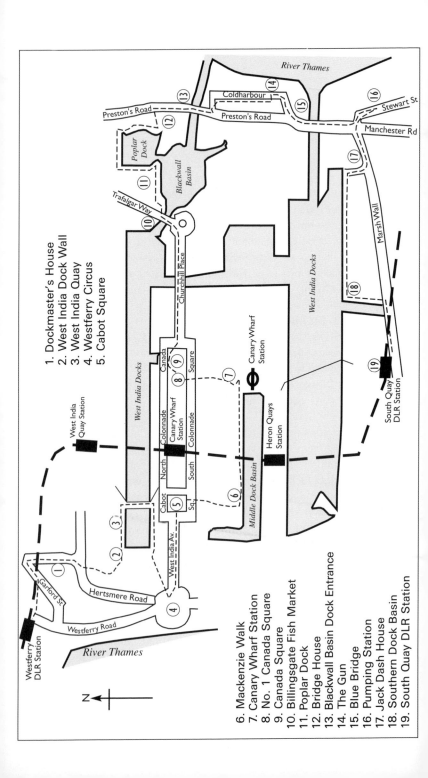

1. Dockmaster's House
2. West India Dock Wall
3. West India Quay
4. Westferry Circus
5. Cabot Square
6. Mackenzie Walk
7. Canary Wharf Station
8. No. 1 Canada Square
9. Canada Square
10. Billingsgate Fish Market
11. Poplar Dock
12. Bridge House
13. Blackwall Basin Dock Entrance
14. The Gun
15. Blue Bridge
16. Pumping Station
17. Jack Dash House
18. Southern Dock Basin
19. South Quay DLR Station

River Thames

Coldharbour
Preston's Road
Preston's Road
Stewart St
Manchester Rd

Poplar Dock
Blackwall Basin
Trafalgar Way

West India Docks

Marsh Wall

Churchill Place

West India Quay Station

West India Docks

Canary Wharf Station

Colonnade
Canary Wharf Station
North Colonnade
South Colonnade

Canada Square

Heron Quays Station

Middle Dock Basin

South Quay DLR Station

Cabot Sq.

West India Av.

Westferry Station

Garford St.

Hertsmere Road

Westferry Road

River Thames

N

inside of Britain's tallest building, No.1 Canada Square, and look down into Norman Foster's exciting Jubilee Line Station which has been described as an Underground Cathedral.

1. DOCKMASTER'S HOUSE

Towards the end of the street on your right is the Dockmaster's House with its fine classical portico, built in 1807. In the past it was used as a tavern and a dock manager's office. Today it is an Indian restaurant.

To the south are two Portland stone gateposts which used to support the main entrance gates to the docks. Dockers would crowd round here hoping to be called for work. Lining the road ahead of you to the left are the Grade I listed West India Quay warehouses. This road used to be known as 'Blood Alley' because the dockers carrying the heavy bags of sugar had the skin of their hands, necks and backs rubbed raw. Today the warehouses have been converted into mixed residential and leisure complexes.

Walk to the right until you come to an opening in the high wall on your left.

2. WEST INDIA DOCK WALL

On the wall to the left of the present-day entrance to the dock is a flowery inscription in praise of the private enterprise which led to the construction of the West India Docks. The docks were opened in 1802 and given a 21-year monopoly over England's trade with the West Indies. The other incentive for building the docks was the cheapness of the land which was marshy and unfit for any other use at the time. Look at the display board which gives more details of the history of the dock, and shows old photographs including one of dockers working in 'Blood Alley' with sugar bags hanging out to dry.

Turn left into the dock.

145

3. WEST INDIA QUAY

The first building you pass on the left, fronted by white Doric columns and a pediment, is the Ledger Building which was used to record all the goods that came in and out of the dock. Today it is one of the many restaurants that line the side of the dock basin. Behind the statue to Robert Milligan, one of the main promoters of the West India Dock Company, is the entrance to the Museum in Docklands. This is housed in the former No. 1 Warehouse where much of the original interior has been preserved for the displays of old dock paraphernalia, photographs and reconstructions of life in the docks.

The dock basin to your right was the northernmost of the three basins excavated for the West India Dock Company. All were excavated by hand. Along the quayside you can see some of the old cranes as well as various boats and sailing barges. This is in stark contrast to the open-air restaurants in front of the warehouses and the towering modern Canary Wharf development across the footbridge. The original western entrance for ships from the Thames was at the far right-hand corner of the basin. You can see a modern replica of the original dock entrance gates with a model ship on top nearby.

Modern model of the entrance gate to West India Docks with the original early nineteenth-century warehouses behind

Now walk over the dock basin via the footbridge, noting how the glass circles under your feet change colour as you pass over them. At the other side, turn right along the path on the south side of the dock basin. At the end go up the steps into Columbus Courtyard. Cross this diagonally past the fountains and large bronze sculpture and follow the sign to Westferry Circus through the arcade. Now walk on into the circular garden area.

4. WESTFERRY CIRCUS

The railings and gates around Westferry Circus garden, designed by British craftsman Giuseppe Lund, symbolise the seasons. Each post of the railings is topped by a floral or foliage pattern. The plantings also reflect the time of year. In summer, for instance, the flower beds glow with bright yellow and orange marigolds. Many birds are attracted by this setting, including falcons and kingfishers. You can see a bird feeder just before the gates facing the river to the west.

Down the steps to the river is Canary Wharf Pier, the landing stage for ferry services to central London and Greenwich. You can also admire Ron Arad's sculpture *Windwand*, which is a 50-metre-high slender red mast designed to sway gently in the wind. It is listed in the *Guinness Book of Records* as the tallest sculpture in the world. Further to the south is Cascades, built in yellow brick as the first large luxury residential development on the Isle of Dogs. The architectural firm CZWG designed it to reflect the maritime theme of the docks. The series of penthouses each with its own terrace and portholes could be construed as a ship.

Go back to Westferry Circus and then into West India Avenue. Walk to the end and into Cabot Square.

5. CABOT SQUARE

You are standing in the centre of the original Canary Wharf development built in the 1980s. This stretched from

Westferry Circus in the west to No. 1 Canada Square, the tall building with the pyramid-shaped top which towers above the block to the east of the square. The variety of architectural styles results from some of the buildings being designed specially for a particular client. One example is the Chicago style of No. 10 Cabot Square, built for Barclays Capital. Many people are surprised to find that this is contemporary with the other more modern-looking buildings here. In fact, all have modern interiors, designed for the age of technology, but differ in their cladding.

Olympia and York, the developers, went into receivership during the depression of the early 1990s, but have been reconstituted as the Canary Wharf Group. This has resulted in the construction of many new office buildings to the south and east as well as a vast expansion of retail outlets.

The name 'Canary Wharf' comes from the former wharf here which handled trade with the Canary Islands. Several of the locations have been given names with Canadian connections because Paul Reichmann, who originated the Canary Wharf development in the 1980s, is himself Canadian. This square is named after John Cabot who sailed from Bristol and discovered Newfoundland and the east coast of Canada in 1497.

The sculpture *Couple on a Seat* at the top of the steps leading down to the dock basin on the north side is by Lynn Chadwick, who was strongly influenced by Henry Moore. In the centre of the square is a fountain controlled by a sensor that measures wind speed and ensures that the height of the water is kept low enough not to spray onlookers. The sensing is performed by the revolving balls on top of the lamppost to the south-west of the square.

From Cabot Square, walk down the steps to the south until you come to the Middle Dock Basin.

6. MACKENZIE WALK

Here you have another view of Cascades diagonally to your right. Nearer to you are a number of low-rise wooden buildings in attractive reddish and purple colours. These were among the first buildings to be constructed here, reflecting the initial enthusiasm for using the Enterprise Zone tax advantages granted to developers by the London Docklands Development Corporation (LDDC) in the 1980s. As land values have risen, they are no longer considered to be economical and it is believed they will be pulled down for redevelopment.

Go to the left along Mackenzie Walk until you arrive at Canary Wharf Station.

7. CANARY WHARF STATION

The station was designed by Norman Foster. Its semicircular glass canopy leads down to the concourse below, which is even longer than No. 1 Canada Square is tall. There is a corresponding canopy at the eastern entrance and together they allow natural light to create a much brighter atmosphere than you find in older Underground stations. It is part of the Jubilee Line extension which opened in 1999, largely in order to provide sufficient commuter capacity for the expanding Docklands business community.

Now walk past the six clocks, which are actually pieces of sculpture designed by Konstantin Grcic, and up the steps to South Colonnade. Cross over and enter No. 1 Canada Square using the swing doors.

8. NO. 1 CANADA SQUARE

Also referred to as Canary Wharf Tower, this is the tallest building in Britain, rising to a height of 800 feet. The architect was Cesar Pelli, who also designed the World Trade Centre which formerly towered over New York. No expense was spared on the materials. On the outside it is clad in 27,500 tonnes of British steel, and inside the lobby the walls are covered with beautiful black, grey, green and red marble from Turkey, Italy and Guatemala. The tower is occupied by

Computer controlled fountains in Cabot Square with No.1 Canada Square towering above

many different firms, including three newspaper publishers – *The Independent*, *Daily Telegraph* and the Mirror Group. On your left you can check the progress of the world's stock markets on the television screens.

Exit the building by the doors to your right into Canada Square and walk to the blue circular structure in the middle of the grassy area.

9. CANADA SQUARE

The centrepiece of Canada Square is the sculpture, *The Big Blue*, by Ron Arad, who also designed *Windwand* on the riverside by Westferry Circus. It is an asymmetrical glass-fibre structure resting on a circular glass ring which lets light into the shopping centre below.

Go to the east end of the square, past Waitrose, and carry on along Churchill Place to Cartier Circle Roundabout.

10. BILLINGSGATE FISH MARKET

The long yellow building on the left is Billingsgate Fish Market, which moved here in 1982 from its historic location north-east of London Bridge in the Pool of London. Although it is primarily a market for fish traders, the public can buy fish here too. There are as yet unconfirmed plans to move the market again to another site in East London.

Looking back you can see No.1 Canada Square framed by two more recent tall buildings. On the left is the Citigroup building, designed by Cesar Pelli, and on the right, HSBC, designed by Norman Foster. As of 2003, construction is still progressing on further buildings here. The foundations have to be dug much deeper than the former dock basins because of the marshy ground, and it seems that almost as much concrete is used to fill the foundations as to construct the building above ground.

Turn left up Trafalgar Way, cross to the right side of the road and descend the steps onto the path by Blackwall Basin. Walk around the north side of the Basin and turn left into Poplar Dock.

11. POPLAR DOCK

This small dock has been converted into a marina. A variety of ships, barges and boats are moored here at an average annual cost of £4,000. The marina is surrounded by apartments and the path around it is lined with old cranes, willow and chestnut trees.

Continue round Poplar Dock until you come to the end of the dock wall on its eastern side where you exit and turn left onto Preston's Road.

12. BRIDGE HOUSE

On your right is Bridge House, built in 1819 by John Rennie, who also designed several bridges over the Thames as well as the London Docks in Wapping. The imposing Georgian brick-built house with its bow windows was the home of the superintendent of the West India Dock Company and is now the headquarters of the

London Federation of Boys' Clubs, whose patron is the Duke of Edinburgh. The wall you have just passed through is part of the original high wall which surrounded the dock to prevent pilfering. It is now a Grade I listed building.

Continue down Preston's Road to where it crosses the water inlet.

13. BLACKWALL BASIN DOCK ENTRANCE

This was the original eastern dock entrance from the Thames. Ships would have to wait here for high tide so that the lock gates could be opened to let them in without the risk of letting out too much water from the dock basins. Today the entrance here is blocked and all shipping goes in by the Blue Bridge which you will come to shortly. Here you have a good view of Canary Wharf to the west and of the Dome across the Thames to the east. Blackwall Basin featured in the ferocious speedboat chase at the start of the Bond film *The World is Not Enough*.

A view of the Dome from the Southern Dock Basin entrance for ships from the Thames

Cross over the old dock entrance and turn left into Coldharbour. Note the two eighteenth-century houses on the left at the beginning of this road. The first, built in yellow brick with an elaborate door case, is called Isle House, and the second, with its Doric columns in front, is called Nelson House. Carry on towards the end of Coldharbour.

14. THE GUN

This pub is built on the site of an earlier inn associated with Lord Nelson, who is said to have used it to meet his mistress, Lady Hamilton. It was said that there was a tunnel between the pub and Nelson House, which you have just passed, although there is some dispute about this. There used to be a foundry here, dating back to the seventeenth century, where guns were made – hence the name of the pub.

From the pub walk away from the river back to Preston's Road and turn left.

15. BLUE BRIDGE

This bridge was built in 1970, not long before the closure of the docks, and today is the only entrance from the Thames. Eighty per cent of the materials used in the development of Canary Wharf were transported through here. The bridge is operated from the British Waterways Office on the other side of the dock entrance. The large rectangular steel structure at the top of the bridge revolves on the arch to raise the bridge when ships pass through.

Just to the north of the bridge on the right side of the road are four curved grey structures leaning together like a quartered orange. This is a ventilation shaft for the Jubilee Line Underground which crosses the Thames at this point and goes on to North Greenwich, the station for the Dome.

Cross the bridge and turn left by the roundabout into Stewart Street.

16. PUMPING STATION

The colourful building with the outsize columns and jet-engine-type fan in its pediment was designed in 1989 by John Outram Associates. The predominant colours are yellow, signifying land, and blue, signifying water. It has won several architectural awards although its seemingly mundane task is to pump storm water from the saturated ground into the Thames to avoid the risk of flooding. Flooding is a constant danger here as the ground was always marshy and now that the industrial use of water has ceased, the water table is rising.

Retrace your steps to the roundabout and cross over into Marsh Wall.

17. JACK DASH HOUSE

The modern building on the right houses departments of Tower Hamlets Borough Council and, in the circular brick section, a small art gallery. It is named after Jack Dash, the communist dockers' leader who led his men on many strikes in the 1960s and 1970s. The docks were always plagued by poor industrial relations and this was one of the causes of the sharp decline which led to their ultimate closure. Jack Dash himself later retrained as a Blue Badge guide and it would have been fascinating to have been on one of his tours of Docklands.

Turn right at the far side of Jack Dash House and go up to the south side of the Southern Dock Basin. Turn left and walk to where the path turns sharply left at the channel that joins West India Dock to Millwall Dock to the south.

18. SOUTHERN DOCK BASIN

Look at the display board showing old photographs of the layout of the three dock basins. This basin was originally a canal whose owners hoped to profit by charging ships a toll to pass through, avoiding the longer river journey to London around the Isle of Dogs peninsular. Most ships preferred to avoid the toll and continued to use the longer route, so in 1829 the West India Dock Company converted the canal into a third basin to handle their expanding business.

Walk along the channel to Marsh Wall, turn right across the bridge and go on to South Quay DLR Station.

19. SOUTH QUAY DLR STATION
On your left are more low-rise buildings which reflect the initial enthusiasm for using the Enterprise Zone tax advantages granted to developers by the LDDC in the 1980s. Just before you reach the station on the right is the site of the IRA terrorist bomb explosion which killed two people and damaged many buildings on 9 February 1996. The resilience of the local business community was shown when people returned to work almost immediately and only one company had to be relocated.

Looking back on the left you can see where the West India Dock linked with the Millwall Dock to the south. The name 'Millwall' comes from the large number of mills which used to operate here by the dock wall. The massive blue-glass structure known as Harbour Exchange was built in 1986 and was the second largest building in Docklands at the time. Further down the Millwall Dock Basin you can see a Chinese restaurant housed in an old Chinese Junk called *Lotus*.

The walk ends here. You can return to your destination via the DLR or walk across the signposted pedestrian bridge to Canary Wharf Station.

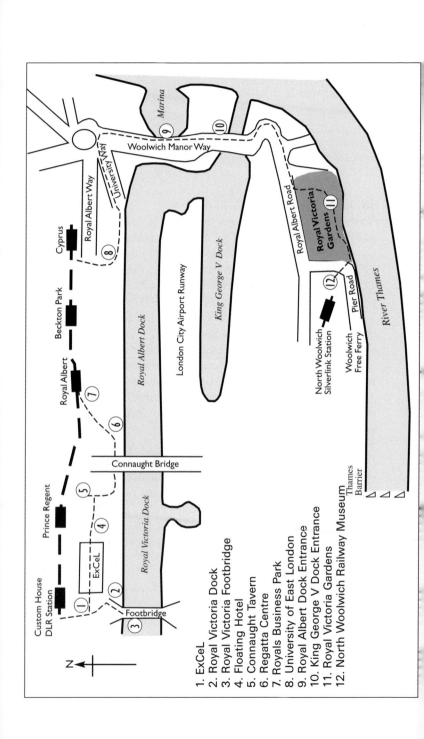

Custom House
DLR Station

Prince Regent

Beckton Park

Royal Albert

Cyprus

N

Marina

Woolwich Manor Way

University Way

Royal Albert Way

ExCeL

Footbridge

Connaught Bridge

Royal Victoria Dock

Royal Albert Dock

London City Airport Runway

King George V Dock

Royal Albert Road

Royal Victoria Gardens

North Woolwich
Silverlink Station

Woolwich
Free Ferry

Pier Road

River Thames

Thames
Barrier

North Woolwich Railway Museum

1. ExCeL
2. Royal Victoria Dock
3. Royal Victoria Footbridge
4. Floating Hotel
5. Connaught Tavern
6. Regatta Centre
7. Royals Business Park
8. University of East London
9. King George V Dock Entrance
10. Royal Albert Dock Entrance
11. Royal Victoria Gardens
12. North Woolwich Railway Museum

The Royal Docks

START: Custom House DLR Station. Follow the signs from the station to the western entrance of ExCeL.

FINISH: North Woolwich Silverlink Station.

WALKING DISTANCE: 2½ miles

HIGHLIGHTS: ExCeL Exhibition Centre, Royals Business Park, University of East London (UEL), the Royal Dock basins.

FOOD & DRINK: ExCeL has a wide variety of cafés and restaurants, and UEL has a cafeteria.

This walk takes you into a world far removed from that of central London. Here the three vast dock basins, which cover 230 acres of water, formed the largest area of inland docks in the world. They were the last to be constructed and the last to close down. The distance from end to end is equivalent to that between Marble Arch and Tower Hill. Following their closure in the 1980s almost all the surrounding buildings were pulled down and all that was left was three long stretches of water. A few historic structures remain, including nineteenth-century warehouses, cranes and the Gallions Hotel where passengers used to stay before boarding their ocean liners. The London Docklands Development Corporation (LDDC), set up by Margaret Thatcher in 1982 to oversee the redevelopment of the docks, itself closed down in 1998, leaving later developments to a variety of planning authorities and Newham Borough Council. By 2004 many of the plans have come to fruition and you will see several exciting modern developments along the waterfront. As the distances are long, you will find it convenient to combine walking with using the DLR from which you have a fine view of Docklands, especially from the right-hand windows as you travel from central London.

1. EXCEL

ExCeL exhibition centre was opened in November 2000 to compete with Earls Court and Olympia for the growing exhibition market. The architects Ray and Mike Moxley designed a rectangular structure stretching half a mile along the north side of the Royal Victoria Dock Basin. The striking white steelwork which holds up the roof allows maximum use of the space as there are no interior supporting columns. The glass pyramid entrance is reminiscent of I.M. Pei's extension to the Louvre. This would seem to be the ideal location for the annual London Boat Show which is expected to take place here in 2004 instead of at Earls Court.

To the west you can see several new hotels, built to serve the exhibitors and visitors. These did not exist when the centre opened and the lack of convenient hotel accommodation resulted in initial financial difficulties for the owners. The modern buildings contrast with the nineteenth-century Grade II listed warehouses which are being converted into mixed-use leisure and office facilities. The smaller 'W' warehouse in front was built in 1880 and the long one behind in 1858. They were mainly used to store tobacco.

Go down the steps to the side of the dock basin.

2. ROYAL VICTORIA DOCK

The Royal Victoria Dock was opened by Prince Albert during the Crimean War in 1855. It was the first dock to use the new railways, the first designed to take the new iron steamships, and the first to use hydraulic cranes. It was an immediate success and by 1860 it handled 40 per cent of all cargo entering the docks on the north side of the Thames. Together with the other royal docks it finally closed in 1981.

The basin was originally excavated by teams of four men using a horse and cart to remove the rubble which was then taken to Battersea to create the park there. Several of the old cranes have been preserved as a striking reminder of the hectic loading and unloading of cargoes that took place here until the 1970s. It took 40 men using winches or treadmills to raise the same amount of cargo that one man could raise here with a crane, and so the availability of cranes gave the Royal Victoria Dock a competitive advantage until the technology was introduced to the other docks.

Go up the stairs or lift to the high-level walkway of the footbridge.

3. ROYAL VICTORIA FOOTBRIDGE

This bridge was designed in 2001 by Lifschutz, Davidson and Techniker to allow access to ExCeL and the DLR from the new Britannia Urban Village on the south side of the dock. Its 11-metre height is sufficient for sailing boats to pass through. From the top you have an excellent overall view of the layout of the Royal Docks and the distance from the City of London to the west.

To the west is a sailing club and windsurfing centre. The original entrance to the dock was at the south-west corner, to the left of the sailing club, but this has now been

Nineteenth-century dock cranes next to the twenty-first-century ExCeL exhibition centre

closed. Further west you can see Canary Wharf and, in the distance, the City of London with the distinctive 'Gherkin' by Norman Foster. To the east is the Connaught Bridge, which marks the division between the Royal Victoria and the Royal Albert docks beyond. You can also see the lights which line the runway of City Airport. On the south side of the dock is the recently developed Britannia Urban Village which has both private and public housing. Next to it is the massive Spillers Millennium Mills, built in the 1930s when 50 per cent of the nation's grain was imported. Today we are self-sufficient in grain and the building is derelict.

Return to the ExCeL entrance and walk through the building to the eastern exit.

4. FLOATING HOTEL

As you come out of ExCeL you see the Sunborn Yacht Hotel on the right. On the other side of the dock is Silvertown Quays which is currently being developed into a residential and leisure complex on the site of the former pontoon dock. A giant aquarium is also planned. Further ahead on the right is a distant view of the stainless steel gatehouses of the Thames Barrier which are often compared with Sydney Opera House. Throughout the centuries London has been more and more at risk from flooding as the land gradually sinks to the south-east and influences like global warming bring increasingly higher spring tides up the Thames. The Barrier was opened by the Queen in 1984 and is designed to protect London from floods until at least 2050. It is one of the engineering wonders of the world, spanning 520 metres across the river. The gates themselves normally lie prone on the riverbed, but can be raised in 30 minutes to an upright position between the gatehouses to stem any dangerously high tidal flow. You can have a much closer view from the Thames Barrier Park which is on the north bank of the Thames on the other side of the Royal Victoria Dock.

Continue straight along the path through the middle of the car park to a roundabout and then along the road past the Ramada Hotel. Turn left at the T-junction where you will find The Fox at Connaught Hotel.

5. CONNAUGHT TAVERN

This hotel was formerly a tavern which stood at the entrance to the docks where dockers came early each morning to be 'called on' for work. It had a licence from 4 a.m. so that people could have a drink to set themselves up for the hoped-for day's work. It is said that a docker had a good chance of getting work if he was in debt to the landlord, who would try and persuade the foreman to hire him so that he could repay his debts. There are numerous accounts of the extraordinary lives and working conditions of the dockers and their families, from the famous 1889 strike for the 'Docker's Tanner' which succeeded in raising the hourly rate to sixpence, to the strikes of the post-war years led by Jack Dash. It was here that he used to climb a tree to address the men.

Now turn back down the road to the side of the dock. Turn left along the waterfront path and follow the sign to the Regatta Centre which is on the other side of Connaught Bridge.

6. REGATTA CENTRE

Following the success of the Royal Victoria Dock, the new Royal Albert Dock, named after Queen Victoria's late husband, was opened in 1880 by the Duke of Connaught. This was the largest dock in the world at the time, with a total length of 2,000 metres. It handled passenger liners and, as refrigeration methods improved, frozen meat, fruit and vegetables became the main cargoes.

The Regatta Centre boathouse was designed by Ian Ritchie Architects. If the 2012 London Olympic bid is successful, the Royal Albert Dock will be the ideal location for the rowing events which require a 2,000-metre course.

On the other side of the dock is City Airport. It is ironic

that this successful new airport uses the former infrastructure of the docks which handled the liners that air travel has now displaced. The runway occupies the strip of land between the Royal Albert and King George V docks which used to be thronged with the liners and their passengers. Today the airport is aimed at the business traveller, providing regular flights to UK and European destinations with a remarkable check-in time of 20 minutes. The DLR is currently being extended to provide improved access from the City and Canary Wharf.

The area by the airport, dominated by the large blue and yellow Tate & Lyle Sugar Refinery with its two tall chimneys, is known as Silvertown. It seems that the name comes from Mr S.W. Silver, who was a successful local industrialist, and not from Tate & Lyle's 'Silver Spoon' sugar products. Sugar was one of the most important imports handled by the docks, and sugar refining produced large profits, some of which went to found the Tate Gallery on Millbank in 1897. Much of the industrial activity around the old docks has now ceased, but Tate & Lyle still employs many local people and remains the largest sugar refinery in Europe.

Turn inland and walk to the left of the Regatta Centre and follow the road for about 300 metres to the Royal Albert DLR Station.

7. ROYALS BUSINESS PARK

The red-brick building near the station was built by the Port of London Authority in 1914 as a refrigeration plant to service surrounding warehouses storing beef shipments from Argentina. During the 1926 General Strike it was feared that the electricity supply might be cut off, but two naval submarines arrived and provided sufficient power from their generators to save the 750,000 carcasses of meat stored in the Royal Docks. The building is currently used as the management office for the Royals Business Park which is now being developed along its mile-long waterfront. The first building is a rectangular glass and steel structure just to the east of the DLR station. At the time of writing, rents here are about £25 per sq ft which is considerably lower than the £45 per sq ft at Canary Wharf and the £60 per sq ft which is common in the City.

Catch the next train and alight at Cyprus DLR Station. Follow the signs to the University and walk through the campus to the edge of the dock.

8. UNIVERSITY OF EAST LONDON

This new campus of the University of East London was designed by Edward Cullinan Architects and opened in 1999. There is a nautical feel to the architecture, especially the colourful circular student accommodation buildings with their portholes and curved roof-tops. The Thames Gateway Technology Centre is housed on the campus to promote contact between the academic and business worlds and to attract new industries. It is hard to remember that as recently as 1998 the whole of the north side of the Royal Albert Dock was an empty, derelict wasteland while now it is lined with modern architecture such as the Regatta Centre, the Business Park and this university campus.

'Pepper-pot' student accommodation at the University of East London, with the Gallions Hotel in the background

Turn left and walk along the side of the dock past the circular student lodgings. At the end turn left to exit the campus via University Way where you will arrive at a roundabout. Here cross Woolwich Manor Way, turn right over the bridge recently renamed after the Olympic rowing champion, Sir Steven Redgrave, and carry on past the marina on the left.

9. ROYAL ALBERT DOCK ENTRANCE

The entrance to the Royal Albert Dock used to be at the end of the marina. To the left, the long grey building is the European headquarters of Norton Healthcare, which has a working relationship with the University of East London Technology Centre. Further left is a red-brick building with a gabled roof and a strange turret on the right. Now disused, this was formerly the Gallions Hotel for the use of passengers about to embark on the ocean liners which set off from the Royal Albert and King George V docks. It is built on stilts and has space for stables below the ground. It is a Grade II listed building, but as yet there are no plans for its use.

Here the Thames starts to curve round the stretch of the Thames known as Gallions Reach towards Beckton. If you look to the left you can see three of the gas-holders of the Gas Light and Coke Company's Beckton gas works, which was the largest in Europe until the introduction of North Sea gas in the 1960s. The works and the new town nearby were named after Simon Adams Beck, the first governor of the company. Production has now ceased and much of the land has been reclaimed for redevelopment along the Thames at Gallions Reach. Two of the surplus gas tanks were blown up for the filming of Stanley Kubrick's *Full Metal Jacket*.

Just out of sight beyond the gas works is Beckton sewage works. This processes all the sewage outflow from London on the north side of the Thames. The main intercepting sewers of Sir Joseph Bazalgette still send their contents here to be turned into 'cakes' that can be burned in power stations. The resulting water is evidently clean enough to be despatched into the Thames. The process was not always so effective, and the original idea was to put the untreated sewage directly into the river at high tide in the hopes that it would be taken out to the North Sea as the tide went out. Unfortunately it all returned up the river when the tide came in again.

To the west you can see the full two-and-a-half-mile length of the royal docks and beyond them the Dome, Canary Wharf and, in the far distance, the City. In the 1980s when there were few buildings and no marina here it would have felt a very lonely place for a visiting walker. Even today you may appreciate the presence of a companion to share the vastness of this remote area of docks.

Continue along Woolwich Manor Way to the bridge over the King George V Dock entrance.

10. KING GEORGE V DOCK ENTRANCE

The entrance from the Thames to the left is still operational and the bridge you are standing on can be raised to allow tall ships to pass through. As of summer 2003 there is a considerable wobble as vehicles pass over, but I was assured by the local management that this was going to be fixed. In the past, ocean liners arrived through this passage, which was only just wide enough for the *Mauretania* as shown in a photograph displayed in the Museum in Docklands.

The King George V Dock was the last to be built and the first to be excavated by machinery. The private companies that owned the docks had run into financial difficulties by the end of the nineteenth century and in 1908 the Port of London Authority (PLA) was set up to control the whole of the tidal Thames and the docks. The PLA started work on the George V Dock in 1912, but completion was delayed by the First World War and it was finally opened in 1921. That same year the chairman, Sir Joseph Broodbank, wrote: 'The future of the Port of London is as secure as any human institution can be.' It took 61 years to prove him wrong, as the King George V Dock was the last to close in 1982.

Continue along Woolwich Manor Way, which bends right past a new housing development. Shortly after the road changes its name to Royal Albert Road you will come to the Royal Victoria Gardens on the left. Go through the park gate, which is 100 metres further along the road, and walk straight across to the riverside.

11. ROYAL VICTORIA GARDENS

The area this side of the Thames is still called North Woolwich although it is now part of the London Borough of Newham. Many of the people who worked in the docks lived in Woolwich on the other side of the river but the existing ferries charged for the crossing. In 1889 the Council instituted a free ferry which used paddle steamers until 1963, when the present drive-on drive-off diesel boats were introduced. The boats are named after Labour politicians of the 1960s. The ferry is still free and there is plenty of room and no waiting for foot passengers, who share the boat with the large lorries you will soon see, usually waiting in long queues. To supplement the ferry, a foot tunnel was built under the river in 1912. You can see the southern entrance, which is the round red-brick building to the left of the Woolwich end of the ferry on the opposite side of the river.

The concrete landing stage to the left of the foot tunnel entrance was the site of the original shipbuilding dock set up by Henry VIII. The royal docks later moved to the west of the ferry. Further to the left you can see some of the buildings of the Royal Arsenal, the oldest and greatest arms factory in England, which originated in the seventeenth century. This now houses Firepower, the Royal Artillery Museum, which tells the story of arms and gunpowder manufacture through the ages. Further left again is Thamesmeade, a large new housing development. The government plans to build over a million new houses in the south-east of England, and many are expected to be built in this area. Hopefully this will coincide with the implementation of at least one of the new bridges proposed by the Thames Gateway River Crossing campaign group.

Turn right and follow the path along the riverside, keeping in front of the concrete wall which you will reach shortly. Where the path bends to the right, go up the steps. Cross over Pier Road.

12. NORTH WOOLWICH RAILWAY MUSEUM

The inscription on the top of the red-brick building indicates that this is North Woolwich Old Station, dating from 1854. It has a gallery between two projecting sections with white stone quoins, Doric columns and rusticated arches. Today it is a museum. However Silverlink trains still operate from the nearby new station.

The walk ends here. You can catch the Silverlink train from the station by the museum which will take you back to DLR and Underground connections. Alternatively, you could carry on to the free ferry and cross to Woolwich. From the ferry you will have a good view of the Thames Barrier. Woolwich Arsenal Mainline Station is about half a mile from the ferry and will take you back to London Bridge Station.

Thames Barrier

CHAPTER 4

Canal Walks

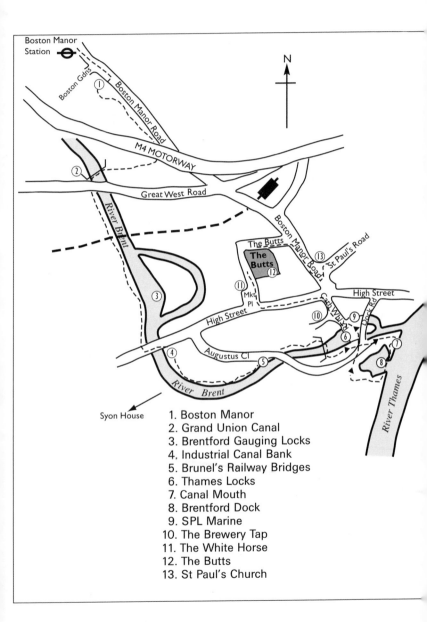

1. Boston Manor
2. Grand Union Canal
3. Brentford Gauging Locks
4. Industrial Canal Bank
5. Brunel's Railway Bridges
6. Thames Locks
7. Canal Mouth
8. Brentford Dock
9. SPL Marine
10. The Brewery Tap
11. The White Horse
12. The Butts
13. St Paul's Church

Brentford

START: Boston Manor Underground Station. Walk about 400 metres down Boston Manor Road until you see Boston Gardens on your right. Continue for a further 100 metres until you reach Boston Manor.

FINISH: St Paul's Church – the nearest station is Brentford Mainline Station.

WALKING DISTANCE: 2½ miles

HIGHLIGHTS: Boston Manor, Grand Union Canal, Brentford Dock, The Butts.

FOOD & DRINK: The Brewery Tap pub and various cafés on Brentford High Street.

Brentford is situated at the confluence of the Thames and Brent rivers and in former times at least one of them could be forded, hence its name. In the eighteenth century the Grand Union Canal was constructed to link London to the industrial Midlands, using the lower reaches of the River Brent to join up with the Thames. After seeing the impressive Jacobean Boston Manor, you will walk along the canalised River Brent past interesting former industrial sites and various locks, both manned and unmanned. At the end of the canal is Brunel's Brentford Dock, now turned into a marina and residential estate with fine views across the Thames to Kew Gardens. Returning from the dock and canal you will find a charming seventeenth-century square known as The Butts – so-called because the area was used for archery in medieval times.

1. BOSTON MANOR

On entering Boston Manor, you will first see the eighteenth-century stable block with its ornate clock tower, which is used as residential accommodation today, before coming to the front façade of the manor house itself.

The house was built in the Jacobean style in 1623 for Lady Mary Reade, whose second husband was Sir Edward Spencer of Althorpe, an ancestor of the late Diana, Princess of Wales. It was extended in 1670. You can see one or other of these two dates inscribed at the top of the various drainpipes which help identify when the different stages of construction took place. The stone portico was added in the nineteenth century. Go round to the back of the house into the surrounding parkland, where you find a lake and several impressive old cedar trees. The large tree on the grassland facing the back façade of the house was planted in the seventeenth century and has the widest girth of any cedar tree in Greater London.

The house was sold to the local council in 1924 when the construction of the Great West Road spoilt the peaceful environs. It is now used partly for residential accommodation and partly for council purposes. The gardens are open daily and the house on weekends and Bank Holidays. Entry is free.

Walk round the left side of the house and then turn left to follow the path through the grounds which runs roughly parallel to Boston Manor Road. When you come to the car park turn sharp right to pass under the motorway and carry on past the vast glass and steel headquarters of GlaxoSmithKline on your left. At the end of the path go through the iron gate which leads up to a footbridge over the canal. Cross to the other side of the canal.

2. GRAND UNION CANAL

The Grand Union Canal was built in the 1790s to link London to the industrial Midlands via the Thames. The canal here in fact makes use of the River Brent. Just over a mile upstream the Brent veers east to its source near Barnet, while the canal continues north-west. Further on at Hayes is the junction with the Paddington arm, which

Milepost showing the distance to Braunston, the northern end of the Grand Junction Canal

was constructed in 1801 to provide a link to the centre of London. The final London link round to Limehouse in the east, known as the Regent's Canal, was completed in 1820.

Upstream you can see that the canal goes by some countrified scenery, while you will walk downstream past a much more industrial landscape. The most modern addition to this is the massive glass-walled GlaxoSmithKline building on the opposite side of the canal with its colourful abstract sculpture dominating the rest area in front. However, in spite of the industrial feel of the canal here, you will still find a surprising variety of bird life, including herons, swans, coots and mallards.

Continue downstream past GlaxoSmithKline and under the Great West Road bridge and then the railway bridge. Note the grooves in the metal rod on the south side of the railway bridge, formed by continuous rubbing by the tow ropes when the barges were pulled along by horses. Walk through the now derelict covered dock to the lock.

3. BRENTFORD GAUGING LOCKS

These locks are unmanned and operated by boat owners themselves using a special key obtainable on application to British Waterways. The River Brent at this point runs behind the island which is currently being redeveloped for residential use. Until 1997 the island was used as a storage depot for the transfer of goods to and from canal barges. The name 'gauging locks' refers to the measuring gauges used to weigh the cargo, in order to calculate the amount of tolls payable before the barges entered the canal here. The sanitary station on your side of the locks is for the use of passing barges, which can moor free of charge for up to 14 days at the iron mooring posts upstream of the lock. The bridge ahead, built in the nineteenth century, takes Brentford High Street over the canal. It marks the spot where the ancient ford over the River Brent was supposed to have been.

Climb the steps up to the High Street. On the opposite side of the road to the left is the fifteenth-century tower of the now deconsecrated Church of St Lawrence, which is Brentford's oldest building. Cross the road, turn left and go down the signposted steps to the canal towpath.

4. INDUSTRIAL CANAL BANK

On your left are some brick arches from the former Brentford Dock Railway which crossed the canal from near where the depth gauge can be seen. The area along the canal here was a hive of industry up to the 1980s. You will shortly pass Albion Timber Merchants, which was a boat repair factory until then. You will also pass several inhabited barges which are attached to electrical and water services.

It is strange to think that behind the trees on the other side of the canal is Syon House, the grand mansion owned by the Duke of Northumberland. The original building dates from the 1540s and Henry VIII's coffin was brought here on its way from Whitehall to Windsor. The coffin burst open during the night and in the morning dogs were found licking up the great King's remains. Syon House was remodelled by Robert Adam in the eighteenth century in the neo-classical style.

Walk along the towpath, ignoring the Thames Path sign which takes you inland, until you come to some iron steps. Go to the upper path here as public access to the lower path ends soon afterwards with a gate which has a sign marked 'Private. Wey Dock'. This sign refers to the former Weigh Dock where cargo loads were calibrated before they went on to the gauging locks you have just passed. You can see the paltry remains of this dock as you start to walk along the upper path. Carry on past the front of the timber merchants. Soon you will come to a road bridge over the canal.

5. BRUNEL'S RAILWAY BRIDGES
The two bridges here were built for the Great Western & Brentford Railway to transport cargo to and from Brentford Dock. They were designed by Isambard Kingdom Brunel and opened in 1859. The bridge over the canal had to be replaced in 1932. The bridge to the left over the road is original. Now the dock and railway are closed, the bridges take road traffic to the new Brentford Dock estate. In front of the bridge is a display board with a map of the area showing the course of the canal.

Turn left off the towpath and pass under the bridge. Then go down the steps back onto the towpath. Shortly you will come to a footbridge over the canal. Cross over and then descend to the towpath on the other side of the canal. Walk on until you come to the locks.

6. THAMES LOCKS
This is the last lock on the canal before it joins the Thames about 300 metres downstream. Barges laden with cargo had access to the Thames here via the Grand Union Canal system from the Midlands and from the north and east of London. The name 'Grand Union Canal' came about after the amalgamation in 1929 of the many

Two narrowboats waiting to pass through Thames Locks

competing, independently owned canals which had been constructed without any consideration of uniform standards. This meant that some sections of the canal were unable to carry larger vessels coming from other sections. The system was nationalised in 1948 and finally came under the control of British Waterways in 1963.

Hardly any freight is transported on the canal today and it is mainly pleasure boats and barges that pass through these locks. The locks were mechanised in 1962 when the lock-keeper's house was rebuilt, and are operated by one of the few, if not only, women lock-keepers employed by British Waterways. The whole area, with its hanging baskets and tubs, is beautifully kept.

Continue along the canal towpath until you reach the River Thames where there are seats with views across the river to Kew Gardens and downstream to the romantic tower of the Kew Bridge Steam Museum.

7. CANAL MOUTH

This is where the canal system finally joins the River Thames. The King's Ferry operated here from the seventeenth to the nineteenth century carrying horses,

Grand Union Canal entering the Thames to the left, with the
tower of the Kew Bridge Steam Museum in the distance

carriages and people to and from Kew on the other side of
the Thames. The landing stage over the river was by what
is now a car park near one of the entrances to Kew
Gardens. Just opposite you, on the banks of the canal, the
largest soap factory in south-east England operated from
1820 until it ceased production in 1961.

Turn right and follow the path by the river until you reach the
lock gates at the entrance to Brentford Dock.

8. BRENTFORD DOCK

The original dock here was built by Isambard Kingdom
Brunel to accommodate boats up to 300 tons in weight.
This whole area was redeveloped in the 1970s when the
old Brentford Dock closed down. The new marina and
surrounding residential apartments replaced the loading
bays, warehouses and railway sidings. The only remaining
industrial activity is boat building.

If the tide is low, you can see all the markings on the
three-metre water-level measure by the lock gates. This
means that the water level in the dock will be considerably

higher than that of the Thames itself. Three metres is roughly the difference between the water level at low and high tide.

Cross the lock gates and walk along the gravel path by the river until you come to a grassy slope which takes you up to the side of the dock. Cross the terrace here and continue to walk inland through the modern housing development until you come to a pink tarmac path. Note the statue of a gardener just ahead of you. You should now turn right along the path past the Brentford Dock Management Office and you will find yourself back at the Thames Locks. Cross over the canal not by Dock Road, but by the black footbridge adjoining the road. On the other side is a boat-building and boat-marketing firm.

9. SPL MARINE

A noticeboard by the offices of SPL Marine shows a list of widely differing boats for sale. Further up the towpath you will cross over two weirs. Normally these weirs flow down to the Thames, but at high tide the flow can be reversed and the water runs back up into the canal. On the left just before the second weir crossing is a yard full of boating materials. This belongs to the firm of Greaves and Thomas, which also has a line in terrestrial and celestial globes.

Follow the path over the two weirs and then up a small road called Catherine Wheel Yard to The Brewery Tap.

10. THE BREWERY TAP

The name 'Catherine Wheel Yard' comes from the Catherine Wheel Inn which used to be here. The present pub was built in 1928 and was popular with the canal community.

Carry on past the pub to the High Street and turn left. Go on to the pedestrian crossing and cross the road into Market Place, past the Courthouse, to The White Horse.

11. THE WHITE HORSE

A market was held at this site from the thirteenth century up to the 1930s. Since then Market Place has been redeveloped and all the buildings are modern. The White Horse is on the site of a previous inn of that name dating from the seventeenth century. J.M.W. Turner came at the age of ten to live in a nearby house with his uncle, who was a butcher. During the four years he spent here he received his first painting commission from a local businessman. He was paid two pence to colour in some pictures of the English countryside. After the death of the businessman his family donated the paintings to Hounslow Library, where they can be seen today.

Walk on to the open square.

12. THE BUTTS

This was originally common land used for archery practice, hence the name 'The Butts', meaning 'targets'. It was enclosed and sold off for building in 1664 and most of the houses survive from that time. They are built of red brick and have decorated wooden door-cases in the fashion of the time. The window frames are flush with the brick fronts. This means that they were built before the 1709 Building Act which established that all window frames should be recessed behind the front wall so as to reduce the risk of fires spreading.

It was here that the hustings for the Middlesex County elections took place in the eighteenth century when the radical politician, John Wilkes, was returned to Parliament several times. Local traders benefited from the two-week campaigns, but the town's reputation suffered from the bribery, brawling, drunkenness and violence that accompanied the elections. Wilkes later attacked the King and his government for corruption in his famously scurrilous tract 'The North Briton'.

There are few other instances where Brentford appeared on the national stage except for two important battles. In 1016 the Danish King Canute defeated the

Saxon King Edmund Ironside and seized his throne, and in 1642 during the civil war, the Cavaliers won one of their few victories against the Roundheads.

Walk diagonally across the square and carry on along the wide avenue until you reach Half Acre at the end. Turn right, cross this road, and then turn left into St Paul's Road.

13. ST PAUL'S CHURCH

You can now see the 1867 tower of St Paul's. The architect, Michael Blee, rebuilt the rest of the church in 1992. It has won many architectural awards. Inside is the painting of *The Last Supper* by Johann Zoffany. This was originally painted for St Anne's Church in Kew, however Zoffany had used local fishermen as models for the disciples and when people started using the disciples' names for the local men, the wife of Judas objected so strongly that the vestry refused to pay for it and it was given to Brentford.

The nearest mainline station is Brentford. Return to Half Acre, turn right and carry on up the main road, which soon becomes Boston Manor Road. In about 400 metres you will come to the station. If you want to return by Underground, continue up Boston Manor Road past the station, cross over the Great West Road and carry on for about half a mile. You will pass Boston Manor itself before you reach the Underground station.

The Regent's Canal

START: Warwick Avenue Underground Station. On leaving the station, walk down Clifton Villas to Blomfield Road where you turn left and shortly come to a bridge.

FINISH: Camden Lock – the nearest station is Camden Town Underground Station.

WALKING DISTANCE: 2¾ miles

HIGHLIGHTS: Little Venice, Regent's Park, London Zoo, Camden Lock Market.

FOOD & DRINK: There are numerous places to eat and drink at Camden Lock Market.

On this walk you will explore part of the Regent's Canal, built in 1820 to complete the link between London and the industrial Midlands. Most of the walk is along the towpath, but there is one small diversion where the canal goes through the Maida Hill Tunnel. You start at the attractive waters of Little Venice where the Regent's Canal joins the Paddington arm of the Grand Union Canal, which was constructed in 1801. Here are brightly coloured inhabited barges on the water and roads lined with fine nineteenth-century stuccoed houses. Further on, you come to a more industrial stretch which reminds you that the original purpose of the canal was to transport goods for commercial and industrial use. Passing under several bridges you then come to another attractive area as the canal passes the north side of Regent's Park and London Zoo. After more reminders of the industrial past the walk ends at the lively Camden Lock Market.

1. LITTLE VENICE

On arriving here, you are faced with the unexpected sight of a large pool of water with an island in the middle,

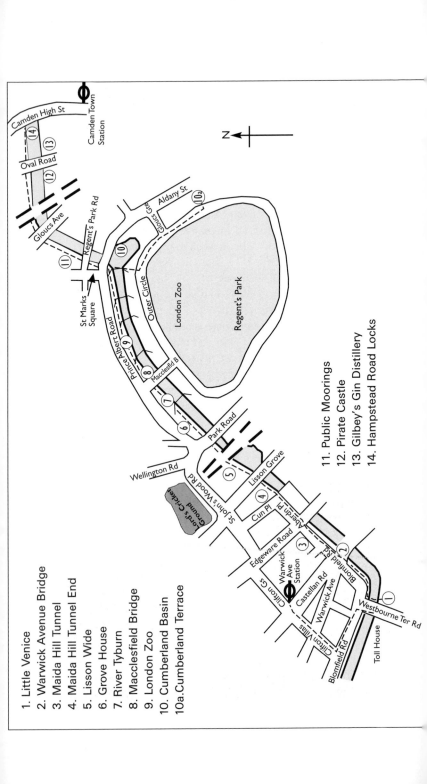

1. Little Venice
2. Warwick Avenue Bridge
3. Maida Hill Tunnel
4. Maida Hill Tunnel End
5. Lisson Wide
6. Grove House
7. River Tyburn
8. Macclesfield Bridge
9. London Zoo
10. Cumberland Basin
10a. Cumberland Terrace
11. Public Moorings
12. Pirate Castle
13. Gilbey's Gin Distillery
14. Hampstead Road Locks

populated by ducks and Canada geese. It is no wonder that the poet Robert Browning, who lived nearby in Warwick Crescent from 1862 to 1867, likened this place to Venice. The pool is also known as Browning's Pool after him. From the bridge you can see where the Paddington arm veers towards Paddington to the south, while the Regent's Canal itself branches to the north-west under the next bridge.

On the other side of the canal and to your right is the former toll house. Here barges had to pay a charge depending on the weight and type of cargo on board. Today it is the office of British Waterways London Region, which controls the canals. It is only a short detour to cross the bridge and descend to the other side of the canal to see if it is open and obtain good-quality free literature about the canals. I especially recommend the series of brochures on the different stretches of the Regent's Canal entitled *London's Canals*.

The houseboats here are wider than the so-called narrowboats you will find on the Regent's Canal to the east. A few are converted commercial boats, but most were purpose-built more recently for homes. They normally cost between £20,000 and £80,000 and the moorings are between £2,000 and £7,000 per annum,

Little Venice with the barge housing Cascades Art Gallery

depending on facilities provided such as mains electricity. They have no engines and never move. To the east of the bridge you can visit the Puppet Theatre Barge and the floating Cascades Art Gallery. Also from here the London Waterbus Company and Jason's Trip run boat trips from Little Venice to Camden Lock and beyond.

Cross back to the original side of the bridge and descend to the towpath. Follow the footbridge back to the left side of the canal. Carry on and pass under the next bridge where the Regent's Canal begins.

2. WARWICK AVENUE BRIDGE

Brightly painted inhabited narrowboats line the towpath to the east of the bridge. Most were built after the canal ceased to be used for commercial traffic. Commercial use declined gradually until it practically ceased in the 1970s. Until well into the twentieth century, horses used the left side of the canal to pull the barges. When engines were introduced in the 1920s the speed limit had to be set at 5 mph to prevent erosion of the banks. The depth of the water is only six feet in the middle and two feet at the sides. Unlike on the early canals, which were too narrow, it is possible for two barges to pass each other here. The international rule is that canal traffic passes on the left. Today you can walk all eight miles along the left-side towpath from here to where it emerges into the Thames at Limehouse, apart from the stretches under two long tunnels. The distance to Camden Lock is two and a half miles.

Carry on along the towpath until the 'Private' sign. Here you must climb up the steps to Blomfield Road.

3. MAIDA HILL TUNNEL

As there is no towpath for the length of this tunnel, horses had to be led over it. The barges were 'legged' through by two men who lay on either side of the barge on planks of wood and pushed it along by use of their feet against the canal wall. This was a laborious and dangerous job, taking about an hour. The introduction of engines reduced this time to two minutes. The spoil from excavating the tunnel was laid on Mr Lord's field, which became Lord's Cricket Ground. This is just to the north of the canal, a few hundred metres further on.

Walk to the end of Blomfield Road, cross Edgware Road into Aberdeen Place. At the end on the corner with Cunningham Place is a sign to the Regent's Canal. Follow this sign to the right and descend the steps to the towpath.

4. MAIDA HILL TUNNEL END

The Maida Hill tunnel ends here, where you will see an information board showing an overall map of the Regent's Canal and you can trace your walk from Little Venice to Camden Lock. There is also a detailed description of the history of the canal. The original idea for the canal came from a businessman called Homer, who was later imprisoned for embezzlement. The architect John Nash, who was a friend of the Prince Regent, was also involved and managed to persuade the Prince to put his name to the canal. In 1812 the Regent's Canal Act was passed and it was finally opened in 1820. Initially it was a great success and soon Thomas Pickford built up a fleet of 120 boats towed by his own horses which were stabled along the canal. After the construction of the Euston terminus in 1837, the railways took away much of the business of the canal. Ironically, the materials for building the station were transported by canal and so it brought on its own downfall.

You may be wondering how the horses managed to return to the towpath here. In fact they had to go on and cross to the other side of the next tunnel ahead of you. Beyond that there is a ramp which allowed them to descend to the side of the canal and then return to pick up the towrope.

The next tunnel under Lisson Grove is short and has a towpath. Look for the grooves where the towing ropes have cut into the metal supports at the bottom of the tunnel entrance. The ropes were made of silk and cotton and were evidently even stronger than most synthetic fibres. There are 40 bridges over the Regent's Canal and you can identify which were built before horses were replaced by engines by seeing if they have these grooves.

Note also the sign on the side of the bridge put up by the former Central Electricity Generating Board warning of the presence of high voltage cables. These were laid under the towpath and further on you will see the paving slabs with handles which cover the cables, as well as many green iron control boxes which also carry a warning.

Walk on under the tunnel where the canal becomes wider for a short distance.

5. LISSON WIDE

The canal here is much wider so that barges could be turned round. This originally had to be done using wind power as the horses could not walk on water. The power station here was built to use coal, which was brought by barges and unloaded into tunnels in the pink wall on your left. The barges then took on ash from the burnt coal for use in brickworks, or manure for farms from the 200 horses stabled here. Today the power station has been converted to gas.

Walk on under two rail and one road bridge. The first two bridges carry the railway to Marylebone Mainline Station and the Bakerloo Line to Baker Street. The third bridge carries Park Road into Regent's Park. Walk as far as the impressive white villa on your left.

6. GROVE HOUSE

Originally one of Henry VIII's hunting grounds, Regent's Park was designed by John Nash with the support of the Prince Regent as the northern part of London's largest urban development scheme stretching from here to St James's Park. Nash was influenced by the contemporary ideas of 'rus in urbe' and created a variety of residential dwellings, clad in gleaming white stucco, surrounded by idyllic parkland and a lake. Not all his plans were realised, as money ran out because of expenditure on the Napoleonic Wars. While most of the planned crescents of terraced houses were constructed and still exist today, only eight of the planned 56 villas were built, of which only four remain.

One of these, Grove House, is on the left side of the canal here. It was designed by Decimus Burton, John Nash's assistant and later a famous architect in his own right, and was recently bought by the Sultan of Oman for £17.5 million. It has the second largest private garden in London after Lambeth Palace. Beyond Grove House to the north of the park are rows of tall red-brick Victorian mansion flats.

On the other side of the canal you can see three large villas in traditional styles, designed by the modern architect Quinlan Terry, who also designed Richmond waterfront. From right to left the styles are Ionic, Italianate and Gothic. Three more villas are currently under construction to the far left. All are being built according to the original designs by John Nash. You may also just manage to see the golden dome of London Central Mosque through the trees to the south.

Walk to the footbridge at the end of the garden.

7. RIVER TYBURN

The Tyburn was one of the three rivers that rose in Hampstead and flowed into the Thames between Victoria and Blackfriars. The others were the Fleet and the Westbourne. All are now covered over. Unlike the Fleet, whose course is now so deep underground that it flows under the Regent's Canal near Camden, the Tyburn is taken over this bridge by an aqueduct, which is concealed in the structure of the bridge.

Walk on to the next bridge.

8. MACCLESFIELD BRIDGE

This bridge is named after the Earl of Macclesfield, the first chairman of the Regent's Canal Company. It is also known as the 'Blow-up Bridge' because of the explosion that took place onboard the narrowboat *Tilbury*, which was laden with gunpowder as it passed under the bridge on 2 October 1874. The three men on board were killed. The bridge was destroyed except for the imposing cast-iron Doric columns which supported it. You can see the word 'Coalbrookdale' imprinted on the top of the capitals. The columns were reused when the bridge was rebuilt. You can see grooves worn by the towropes on both side of the columns. This is because they were erected the other way around, so that the old grooves made before the explosion are on the land side, and the newer ones are on the canal side.

Walk on and pass under the next footbridge.

9. LONDON ZOO

The Zoological Gardens were first laid out in 1828 in this northern section of Regent's Park by Decimus Burton. Animals were transferred here from the royal menageries of Windsor and the Tower of London. As well as being a major tourist attraction, it prides itself on being a centre of research into the welfare and preservation of wild animals. On the other side of the canal you can see oryx and bush pigs. On this side is the modernistic aviary designed by Lord Snowdon, Princess Margaret's first husband. The small birds inside seem dwarfed by the vast space, although they would doubtless like to escape to join their fellows, who can often be seen sitting on top of the aviary. The main entrance is via the next footbridge. There is a special landing on the opposite side for canal boat users who have bought a combined ticket.

Carry on under two more bridges to where the canal branches left and right.

10. CUMBERLAND BASIN

What strikes the eye first here is the Chinese boat/restaurant looking like a pagoda. It is sited on the right-hand branch of the canal, which is now a dead end.

Grooves cut into the side of the bridge by ropes when barges were towed by horses

John Nash originally planned to run the canal through the middle of Regent's Park, but residents opposed this as they did not want rough canal workers disturbing their elegant surroundings. Cumberland Basin used to take the canal as far as Gloucester Gate just to the north of Cumberland Terrace, which is the most magnificent of all the Nash terraces around Regent's Park. If you wish to make a detour to see it, go up the steps and cross the bridge into Outer Circle. Turn left and you will find it in about 400 metres on your left. Its splendid white stucco façade is decorated with porticoes, a central pediment and an array of statues on top.

Return to where the canal branches left, and pass the early twentieth-century Gothic Church of St Mark on the left. The first bridge you come to has no grooves and therefore must be relatively recent, but the second one does have them. Carry on under this bridge to where there is a sign giving the rules for mooring boats here.

11. PUBLIC MOORINGS

This area is available for travelling boats. You can moor here free for 7 days at a time and 14 days in total in any single year. There are no facilities. Narrowboats will normally carry Calor gas and have their own toilets, which can be emptied at sanitary stations. Electricity is generated by the barges' engines. Here is also a plaque recording the existence of a ramp which allowed an escape route for horses that fell into the canal when frightened by the trains passing over the railway bridge ahead. British Waterways have recently removed the ramp, presumably for safety reasons and to allow more space for mooring.

Carry on under Gloucester Avenue Bridge and the two railway bridges built by George Stephenson to take the trains into Euston Station.

12. PIRATE CASTLE

The Pirate Castle, designed by Richard Seiffert and Partners, was built in 1977 as a club to enable local children to enjoy water sports. It owns two narrowboats which can usually be seen nearby. If any children are in them they will enjoy waving to you. The ruined hulk on the right before you reach the castle was a Thames Lighter, which was much wider than the narrowboats. It transported cargo on the Thames and amazingly could be driven by a single lighterman with a long oar. On the left side of the canal opposite the Pirate Castle is a matching castellated structure which is actually a pumping station for pumping water through the high voltage cable ducts to keep the cables cool.

Walk under Oval Road Bridge by the Pirate Castle.

13. GILBEY'S GIN DISTILLERY

On the opposite side of the canal is a white building which used to house Gilbey's Gin Distillery. The foundations were made of cork to protect the cellars from vibrations caused by the trains. The distillery has now been converted into flats and offices. On this side is the former Rail Interchange

Warehouse, which is a listed building about to be converted into residential and leisure use. The towpath rises over the entrance to the basement level landing stage where goods were transferred between rail and canal.

Continue along the towpath to your final destination.

14. HAMPSTEAD ROAD LOCKS

The locks are still known as Hampstead Road Locks even though the main road here was renamed Chalk Farm Road many years ago. The two-storeyed section of the castellated lock-keeper's cottage dates from 1815. The locks themselves are the only remaining paired locks on the Regent's Canal and are the first of 12 locks which take the water level down 85 feet to the outflow into the Thames at Limehouse. The distance to Limehouse is six miles, as shown on the signpost by the locks. Other distances shown include two and a half miles to Little Venice, 146 miles to Birmingham and 302 miles to Liverpool.

Camden Lock Market opened in 1973 on the site of an old timber wharf and dock. Goods of all sorts are on sale here and the market really comes alive at weekends. The lively atmosphere spills out onto the surrounding streets

Hampstead Road Locks with the lively Camden Lock Market

where converted stables now house artists and craftsmen. Anything goes, from body piercing to portrait painting and from food stalls to restaurants.

The nearest Underground station is Camden Town. Climb the steps up to Camden High Street, turn right and you will find the station in about 200 metres on the left-hand side.

CHAPTER 5

Hidden River Walks

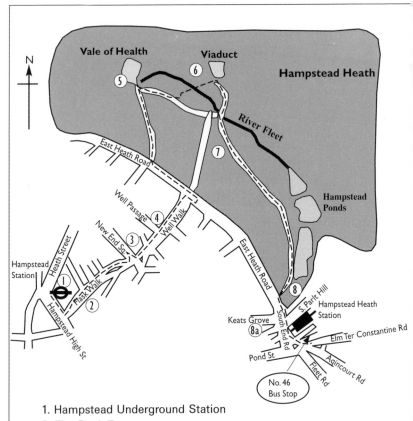

1. Hampstead Underground Station
2. The Flask Tavern
3. Burgh House
4. Fountain
5. Vale of Health
6. Viaduct
7. MoD Ammunition Dump
8. Hampstead Ponds
8a. Keats House
9. St Pancras Old Church

The Fleet River Source

START: Hampstead Underground Station.

FINISH: St Pancras Old Church – the nearest station is King's Cross.

WALKING DISTANCE: 1½ miles

HIGHLIGHTS: Burgh House, Viaduct, Hampstead Ponds, St Pancras Old Church.

FOOD & DRINK: The Flask Tavern, Burgh House café, various restaurants and cafés near Hampstead Ponds.

Three of London's hidden rivers have their sources in the hills of Hampstead. The Westbourne and Tyburn rivers today flow completely underground as overflow sewers and only emerge when they enter the Thames at Chelsea and Pimlico respectively. The River Fleet also runs mainly underground, but you will trace its early stages overground on this walk. You begin in the streets and alleyways of Hampstead village where in the eighteenth-century crowds flocked to take the waters at the chalybeate springs. These have long since dried up, but when you come to Hampstead Heath you will see the embryonic River Fleet emerge from a pond at the Vale of Health. You then walk through the natural wooded countryside of Hampstead Heath following the course of the river, which feeds three large ponds at the bottom of the Heath before disappearing underground through a grille. It is possible to continue the walk tracing the underground course of the Fleet from here, but there is little of interest to see, so I recommend taking a bus to St Pancras Old Church where you find the next outward sign of the river – an eighteenth-century engraving showing people bathing in the Fleet with St Pancras Church in the background.

1. HAMPSTEAD UNDERGROUND STATION

Hampstead prides itself in having a distinctive village atmosphere. It is situated high above London and therefore has the deepest Underground station, descending 192 feet below street level. On the opposite side of the road is a reminder of the past – a building with a clock tower which was once a fire station in the days of horse-drawn vehicles.

Walk down Hampstead High Street, turn first left into Flask Walk and continue along this shop-lined alleyway to The Flask Tavern.

2. THE FLASK TAVERN

This pub was built on the site of the eighteenth-century tavern where water from the nearby spa was sold in bottles, hence the name of the alleyway and tavern. Samuel Richardson describes the tavern in his novel *Clarissa* as 'a place where second-rate persons are to be found, often in a swinish condition'. Evidently spa water was not the only drink consumed there then.

Continue along Flask Walk past the former bathhouse, which has now been turned into residential accommodation, until you come to the junction with New End Square.

3. BURGH HOUSE

It is worth making the short detour to your left up New End Square to see Burgh House, a Grade I listed building, which was built in 1703. This is now a community arts centre and houses the Hampstead Museum of Local History and a café.

Returning to Flask Walk you will find that its continuation is called Well Walk. No. 14 on the right-hand side of the road has a plaque to Marie Stopes, who founded the birth-control organisation named after her. It was here that she lived with her first husband while she wrote her controversial book *Married Love*. The book was banned in the USA because it implied that women could have sex for pleasure and not just to bear children. It seems that Marie Stopes's own marriage was never consummated so the book was based on academic research rather than practical experience.

Continue up Well Walk until you reach a narrow passage on your left called Well Passage.

4. FOUNTAIN

This was the location of the chalybeate springs where crowds came in the eighteenth century to take the medicinal waters. Just opposite, as described on the plaque on No. 46/48, was the Pump Room. As a result of this activity Hampstead changed from being a rather ordinary village into a fashionable spa resort. It attracted famous artists and writers, including John Constable who lived in No. 40 and painted scenes of Hampstead Heath. A blue plaque marks his house. The spa ceased to function in the nineteenth century but Hampstead still retains its reputation as a fashionable place to live, especially for rich left-wing intellectuals. Certainly the wealthy

The stone structure erected to commemorate the chalybeate spring, where Hampstead Spa was set up in the eighteenth century

inhabitants have used their influence to maintain the natural beauty of the Heath, which has been continually under threat from developers over the last 200 years.

Walk to the end of Well Walk and cross East Heath Road to the side of the Heath. Go into the Heath, where there are two paths. One leads straight on downwards. The other is about 100 metres to your left along East Heath Road and leads diagonally to the left. Follow the one to the left until you come to a pond.

5. VALE OF HEALTH

At last you have reached the source of the River Fleet. It has to be admitted this is not very dramatic as all you see is a stone cover at the corner of the pond just by the path. This is where the river trickles rather than flows out of the pond and under the path you were following. The area is known as the Vale of Health after the former spa. The pond was made in the eighteenth century by the Hampstead Water Company as a reservoir to supply water to the City of London. Today the whole of Hampstead Heath is administered by the City Corporation although water is no longer supplied from here.

The trickle of water here gradually increases into a stream as it is joined by various other small tributaries along your walk. There is another major source at Kenwood which does not join up with this river course until they both converge at Camden Town. In 1826 it was recorded that the river there was 65 foot wide during a flood.

Turn down the small path to your right off the path you were following. On the left by a yew tree you can see the initial stages of the river course as it descends through the woods to the valley below. Carry on along the path until you reach an open grassy space. Turn left here across the grass and walk down to a small bridge which crosses the still embryonic river. Carry on over the bridge and up the steep slope on the other side.

6. VIADUCT

Here is the surprising sight of a high red-brick-and-stone viaduct over a large pond where you will often see ducks amid the water lilies. This peaceful scene belies the vicious quarrels between the original Lord of the Manor, Sir Thomas Maryon Wilson, and local residents over his attempts to develop houses around here in the eighteenth century. He did manage to build this viaduct to provide access for coaches to the villas that he intended to build, but then failed to get the necessary parliamentary approval to build the villas themselves. As a result he was forced to sell the land to the Metropolitan Board of Works and so the natural landscape of the Heath has been preserved. From the pond flows another tributary of the Fleet and you can see this going downhill through the woods.

Walk down the path to the right of the direction you came and keep to the left of the stream. Carry on until you reach a bridge where the stream joins the original course of the Fleet. Pause here and look at the flow, which is now much stronger as it passes under the bridge. Now follow the path to the right of the river and up to a wide open area.

7. MOD AMMUNITION DUMP

During the Second World War there was an ammunition dump near here. If it has rained you may see the telltale signs of oil pollution in the puddles on the path. Pollution from all sorts of rubbish was the main cause of the demise of the Fleet's lower stretches and it is fortunate that the same problem has not occurred in this stretch despite the ammunition dump. After heavy rains much water does flow down into the river valley, bringing a considerable amount of debris with it, but as it is mainly organic matter it has no significant effect.

Carry on along the path down to the three large ponds. Walk along the right side to the end of the bottom pond.

8. HAMPSTEAD PONDS

These ponds are fed by the River Fleet and are the last sign of the river you can see above ground. The volume of water here is huge and much appreciated by the many willow trees. Today the uppermost pond is used for mixed bathing. A raft in the middle of the lower pond is often occupied by cormorants who challenge the fishermen for their catch. The ponds attract a wide variety of wildfowl which are unaware of the potential danger lurking behind the grille you can see at the end of the pond about 50 metres from the shore. It is here that the River Fleet disappears for good and flows under the ground as an overflow sewer. This means that it takes the surplus water from rain storms down into the Thames thus avoiding problems with the disposal of domestic and commercial sewage via the main sewers.

Across East Heath Road and a little way up Keats Grove is Keats House where the poet lived for two years. A plaque in the garden records the spot under a plum tree where he wrote his *Ode to a Nightingale*.

East Heath Road becomes South End Road which you now follow past Hampstead Heath Station to South End Green.

Grille at the bottom of Hampstead Ponds where
the River Fleet disappears underground

You can carry on down Fleet Road to the south if you wish to follow the whole course of the Fleet on foot. However there is little of interest for much of this part of the river course. I suggest you turn left at the main road here where you will find the bus stop for the No. 46 bus on the left-hand side. Catch this bus and ask for St Pancras Hospital. When you alight at this stop, you will find St Pancras churchyard just past the hospital on the left side of the road. Go in the second entrance at the church.

9. ST PANCRAS OLD CHURCH

Just behind the beautiful wrought iron entrance gates of the church you can see an eighteenth-century picture of people bathing in the River Fleet as it flows past the church. By now the two main sources at Hampstead and Kenwood have joined up so the river is much wider than it was when you saw it earlier. The total length was six miles from source to its mouth at Blackfriars and it was the largest of the many tributaries of the Thames in the central London area. The upper reaches were not covered over until well into the nineteenth century, some time after the lower reaches as you will discover on the next walk.

The church itself has Norman-style rounded arches and dates from medieval times although it has been heavily restored. It was built on the site of a much earlier sixth-century Saxon church which is considered to have been one of the oldest Christian sites in Britain. Unfortunately you cannot normally enter the church, but the churchyard has many fine monuments to famous people. Behind the church to the left is an old tree surrounded by tombstones and an iron fence. A plaque records that the novelist Thomas Hardy worked here when the Midland Railway Company built its railway on the eastern part of the churchyard and bodies had to be disinterred.

The elegant mausoleum in the centre of the churchyard which is also surrounded by an iron fence was designed by the architect Sir John Soane for his wife. He himself was later buried here as well. If the shape seems familiar it is because it inspired Sir Giles Gilbert Scott's design of

St Pancras Old Church viewed from
where the River Fleet used to flow

the red telephone box. The monument was vandalised in
the 1990s and the restoration unfortunately is rather
obvious as the stone has a different colour from the
original. Other monuments include the tall Victorian
Gothic memorial to the philanthropist Angela Burdett-
Coutts and the plain tombstone dedicated to Mary
Wollstonecraft Godwin, feminist and mother of Mary
Shelley, the author of *Frankenstein*.

The Fleet flows on to King's Cross where the next walk
begins. Currently extensive construction work connected
with the new Channel Tunnel terminus prevents you from
following its underground course in that direction, so you
should take the bus from the stop where you alighted
outside St Pancras Hospital. This will take you safely to
King's Cross Station.

The Fleet River Mouth

START: King's Cross Station.
FINISH: Blackfriars Bridge – the nearest station is Blackfriars.
WALKING DISTANCE: 2½ miles
HIGHLIGHTS: Mount Pleasant, The Clerk's Well, Ely Place, the
    Fleet mouth at Blackfriars Bridge.
FOOD & DRINK: Several restaurants and cafés in the King's
    Cross, Clerkenwell and Fleet Street areas, The Black Friar
    pub.

On this walk you will see no actual river until you reach
the Thames at Blackfriars where there is an arch in the
river wall from which the now-buried River Fleet
emerges. However, there are many reminders of the past
when the Fleet played an important part in the history of
London. The valley of the former river downstream from
King's Cross was fed by many wells, which you will
encounter either in street names, plaques or, in the case of
the Clerk's Well, the real thing. Along the way you will
pass many historic places connected with the river. In Ely
Place is the thirteenth-century St Etheldreda's Chapel, the
only remaining part of the former London palace of the
Bishops of Ely, whose gardens bordered the river. Less
salubrious riverside sites included the huge rubbish dump
known euphemistically as Mount Pleasant, and
Smithfield Meat Market from where the remains of
slaughtered animals falling down into the valley were a
major cause of pollution. South of Fleet Street, named
after a bridge over the river, you pass the sites of Henry
VIII's Bridewell Palace and of Blackfriars Monastery,
which were connected by another bridge over the river.
The walk ends on the Thames Path under Blackfriars
Bridge where in Roman times there was a tidal inlet about
600 feet wide, but today just the sewer outlet remains.

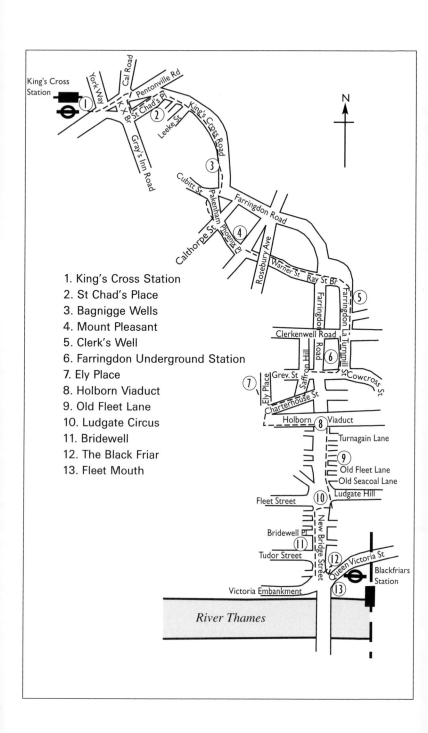

King's Cross Station

York Way

Cal Road

Pentonville Rd

St Chad's Pl

K X Br

Leeke St.

Gray's Inn Road

King's Cross Road

Cubitt St.

Calthorpe St.

Pakenham St.

Phoenix Pl.

Farringdon Road

Rosebury Ave

Warner St.

Ray St Br

N

1. King's Cross Station
2. St Chad's Place
3. Bagnigge Wells
4. Mount Pleasant
5. Clerk's Well
6. Farringdon Underground Station
7. Ely Place
8. Holborn Viaduct
9. Old Fleet Lane
10. Ludgate Circus
11. Bridewell
12. The Black Friar
13. Fleet Mouth

Farringdon Road

Farringdon La.

Turnmill St.

Clerkenwell Road

Cowcross St.

Ely Place

Grev. St.

Saffron Hill

Charterhouse St.

Holborn Viaduct

Turnagain Lane

Old Fleet Lane

Old Seacoal Lane

Ludgate Hill

Fleet Street

New Bridge Street

Bridewell Pl.

Tudor Street

Queen Victoria St

Blackfriars Station

Victoria Embankment

River Thames

1. KING'S CROSS STATION

This area used to be called 'Battle Bridge', but was renamed King's Cross in 1836 after a 60-foot high monument to George IV. The origin of the original name is obscure. It is certain that there was an arched brick bridge over the Fleet in the vicinity, while legend has it that the battle was the defeat of Queen Boudicca by the Romans in AD 61. It is said that she is buried under Platform 7 in King's Cross Station. The station was completed in 1854 as the London terminus for the Great Northern Railway. The original station building remains, fronted by an elegantly simple arched façade of yellow London brick. The clock on the central tower is one of the few visible remnants from the Great Exhibition of 1851, sponsored by Prince Albert with the aim of showing off the wonders of the Industrial Revolution. The Great Exhibition was held in Hyde Park in an enormous iron and glass 'Crystal Palace' and was visited by over six million people. The Crystal Palace itself was later re-erected in Sydenham in south London and proved a great tourist attraction until it burnt down in 1936.

Turn left out of the station, cross York Way and continue along Pentonville Road to the pedestrian crossing where you cross the road into the short road called King's Cross Bridge. Take the first left into the narrow St Chad's Place. Walk as far as the wall over which you can see the railway entering King's Cross Thameslink Station.

2. ST CHAD'S PLACE

It is hard to believe that this unprepossessing area was once the site of a medicinal well dedicated to St Chad, who is supposed to have been cured by drinking waters similar to those that sprang from the well here. It became a popular spa in the eighteenth century, but later went into a gradual decline until it was demolished in 1863 in order to build the Metropolitan Line. This was the world's first underground line, taking passengers in steam trains from Paddington to Farringdon Station. It was constructed by the 'cut and cover' method which involved cutting out a channel to lay the tracks below ground level and then covering it over. Later, much deeper underground lines were excavated using tunnelling machines.

Today the tracks service both the Underground and Thameslink Mainline Railways. In fact the Thameslink trains run from here more or less along the east side of the Fleet valley as far as Blackfriars, where they cross the Thames. As you continue your walk you will notice how the ground slopes down to where the river used to flow even though the ground level is much higher today. The actual course of the river here was slightly to the west of King's Cross Road although it is not possible to follow it precisely because of subsequent building work. Further down, the course follows Farringdon Road almost exactly.

At the end of St Chad's Place turn right onto King's Cross Road. Note the sign to Smithy's Wine Bar, which is in the former bus company stables at the end of the cobbled alleyway called Leeke Street. Carry on for about 600 metres, and then soon after passing a garage you will arrive at No. 61 King's Cross Road where you will see a stone inscription just behind the bus stop.

3. BAGNIGGE WELLS

This was another of the spas which became popular in the eighteenth century although surprisingly the inscription is dated 1680. This is probably because Nell Gwynne was said to have entertained Charles II here well before the medicinal qualities of the water had been discovered. The road opposite is appropriately called Gwynne Place. The spa was opened in 1758 and was an instant success. In a song published in the *London Magazine* in 1759 people were exhorted to 'Obey the glad summons, to Bagnigge repair, drink deep of its streams, and forget all your care.' The River Fleet flowed through the gardens of the spa, and one of the reasons for its popularity may have been the seats provided on the riverbanks for those who wished to consume

Idiosyncratic inscription
denoting the site of
Bagnigge Wells

stronger drinks. Just behind the Bagnigge Wells site are Wells Square and Fleet Square, but unfortunately these days it cannot be said that anything other than the names remind you of the river or the spa.

The stone inscription also mentions The Pindar of Wakefield pub, which is now called The Water Rats and is situated a short way down Gray's Inn Road from St Chad's Place. This historic pub was a favourite with Lenin when he stayed in this area in 1902.

Turn right into Cubitt Street, then left into Pakenham Street. Walk on to the main road at the top of the hill and cross over into Phoenix Place. Walk down this road to Mount Pleasant.

4. MOUNT PLEASANT

The large building on your left is the Royal Mail Mount Pleasant sorting office, built on the site of the former Cold Bath Fields Prison which was demolished in 1889. The prison walls edged the riverbanks. Cold Bath Fields was named after a well of cold water discovered in 1697 and the name is preserved in Cold Bath Square, which is on the south corner of Mount Pleasant and Farringdon

Road. The prison had a bad reputation as described in *The Devil's Thoughts* by Southey and Coleridge:

> As he went through Coldbath Fields he saw
> A solitary cell;
> And the Devil was pleased, for it gave him a hint
> For improving his prisons in Hell.

Until 2003 the famous Post Office Railway operated through here underground, taking mailbags between the various London sorting offices. For financial reasons it has now been closed, which seems a strange decision in view of the attempt to reduce traffic by the introduction of the congestion charge.

The name 'Mount Pleasant' is ironic and refers to a mound of rubbish piled high on the site to the west of the sorting office which was conveniently just outside the boundaries of the City. This is commemorated by the name of nearby Laystall Street which is to your right past the row of eighteenth-century terraced houses on which you can see a plaque with the date 1720. Laystall means a rubbish dump. The problem was that if it rained, rubbish was washed down into the river.

London's middle level intercepting sewer, built in the nineteenth century by Sir Joseph Bazalgette, runs under where you are standing. The waters of the Fleet enter this large tunnel and help flush the sewage to the processing plant at Beckton to the east of London. Only if the rain is heavy does the surplus water actually flow out of the intercepting sewer to reach the Thames.

Cross Mount Pleasant into Warner Street, then go along Ray Street to Farringdon Road. From here the river follows the main road to Blackfriars, but you can take several detours to make the walk more interesting. Cross over Farringdon Road and go up the short Ray Street Bridge and turn right into Farringdon Lane. Soon on your left is the window of No. 16 through which you will see a water pump and an inscription about the Clerk's Well.

5. CLERK'S WELL

This well is mentioned among others in the Fleet valley area by William Fitzstephen, Thomas à Becket's secretary, in his account of London written in 1174. He records that the water was 'sweet, clear and salubrious'. In medieval times people came to these wells for supplies of free water and to socialise. As few could read, mystery plays were performed by various guilds to provide education about the Bible stories. Mystery in fact comes from the French word *métier*, meaning craft. The parish clerks performed here, and so the district was, and still is, called Clerkenwell. Look through the window to the right and you will see a picture of the clerks performing the expulsion of Adam and Eve from the Garden of Eden. There is also a blown-up version of the sixteenth-century map of the area, known as the AGAS map, showing the Clerk's Well and the River Fleet to the west.

The well was lost during construction work in the nineteenth century, but was uncovered by more rebuilding in 1924. Today it can be visited by special request.

Go to the end of Farringdon Lane, cross Clerkenwell Road and continue on down Turnmill Street to Farringdon Underground Station.

6. FARRINGDON UNDERGROUND STATION

As you have just come down Turnmill Street it is worth mentioning that the River Fleet was sometimes called Turnmill Brook because of the many mills operating here along its banks. It was also popular as the site of breweries and gin distilleries. Booths built its distillery at the top of Turnmill Street in 1778 when the river was still open at this point. It continued operation until the 1980s, long after the river had disappeared underground.

Despite many attempts to clean it up, pollution of the Fleet was a continual problem until it was eventually covered up. The enclosure of the lower stretch from Holborn Viaduct to the Thames was carried out in the eighteenth century, while the upper reaches were gradually covered during the nineteenth century. The pollution had many causes, including the construction of latrines over the river, industrial usage by mill owners, and rubbish of all sorts being dumped into the river. Smithfield Market, which is about 200 metres along Cowcross Street to your left, was a major cause of the latter. Jonathan Swift in his poem *A City Shower* writes of 'Sweepings from Butcher's stalls, dung, guts and blood' falling into the river. However *The Gentleman's Magazine* recorded some benefit. A boar was lost for a month before finally emerging from the Fleet ditch (now a sewer) at Blackfriars much fatter and improved in price from ten shillings to two guineas.

Even after it had been turned into an underground sewer, the river was a constant source of danger because of the build-up of noxious gases. In 1862 it exploded and burst into the newly constructed railway at Farringdon, causing serious damage and filling the tunnel with sewage. The vastly improved system of sewers built by Sir Joseph Bazalgette seems to have solved this particular problem.

Turn right into Cowcross Street and then cross Farringdon Road into Greville Street on the opposite side. Turn left into Saffron Hill, walk to the end and then climb the steps up to Charterhouse Street where you turn right and shortly see some fine wrought iron gates on your right.

7. ELY PLACE

Behind the gates is Ely Place, a row of fine eighteenth-century town houses, built on the site of the great London palace of the Bishops of Ely. It overlooked the Fleet valley with its gardens, which are mentioned as having fine strawberries in Shakespeare's *Richard III*. Even today there is an annual Strawberrie Fayre held every June.

The only evidence of the palace today is St Etheldreda's Chapel, halfway up Ely Place on the left-hand side. You can visit this unusual church, which dates from the thirteenth century. It has a crypt and an upper church and the walls of both are largely original. The inside was restored after bomb damage, and the stained-

Ely Place, site of the Bishop of Ely's Palace which
overlooked the River Fleet until Tudor times

glass windows are remarkable. The West Window is the
largest stained-glass window in London, covering an area
of 500 square feet, which is surprising, as the church
seems rather small from the outside.

Leave Ely Place, cross Charterhouse Street and turn left into
Holborn Viaduct. Stop when you come to the bridge.

8. HOLBORN VIADUCT

The viaduct was opened by Queen Victoria in 1869 at the
same time that she opened the new Blackfriars Bridge.
The dramatic Victorian architecture is best seen from
below, but here you can admire the four bronze statues
representing on the north side Commerce and
Agriculture, and on the south side Science and Fine Arts.
It was designed to allow traffic easier access between the
City and Holborn, avoiding the steep descent into the
valley of the Fleet where it was bridged at the level of the
river. Downstream from here the river was covered over in
the eighteenth century.

The name Holborn derives from one of the old names
of the Fleet – Holebourne, or stream in the hollow. This

refers to the distinct valley through which it flows in its lower courses. The alternative explanation, that it refers to a tributary which joined the Fleet here, is unlikely.

Cross to the south-east side of the viaduct and go down the steps. Walk down Farringdon Street as far as Old Fleet Lane. On the way you will pass Turnagain Lane, where it was necessary to 'turn back again' in the days when the river was here because there was no bridge over it.

9. OLD FLEET LANE

To your left is a modern development, Fleet Place, built on the site of the old Fleet Prison which was opened in the twelfth century and only closed in 1844. Many important people were imprisoned here and it was particularly known as a prison for debtors. It was here that Charles Dickens has Mr Pickwick imprisoned for breach of contract when he refuses to marry his landlady, who mistakenly assumed he had made an offer of marriage. The prison was also notorious for the so-called 'Fleet marriages', which were conducted clandestinely by clergymen imprisoned for debt. This practice was stopped by an Act of Parliament in 1733. In the same year a fruit and vegetable market was set up when the stretch of river between Holborn Viaduct and Ludgate Circus was covered over. This lasted into the nineteenth century.

Walk on to Ludgate Circus, passing Old Seacoal Lane on your left. This name refers to the coal which was shipped via the North Sea up the Thames to be landed here. It was the tax on this coal which helped finance the rebuilding of the City after the Great Fire of 1666.

10. LUDGATE CIRCUS

To your left is Ludgate Hill with a view of St Paul's Cathedral. Sir Christopher Wren cleaned up and widened the Fleet River after the Great Fire of 1666 had destroyed all the houses and wharves on either side, and the stone for the rebuilding of St Paul's was shipped from Portland in Dorset and landed near here. Unfortunately the river soon deteriorated and by 1766 was totally covered.

Fleet Street marks the place where Fleet Bridge crossed the river. This was the main route between the City and Westminster. Not surprisingly, Fleet Street was chosen by the proprietors of the newspaper industry to set up their presses as it was so central and linked the trading world of the City to the Government in Westminster. A plaque on the north-east corner of Ludgate Circus marks the publication of the first newspaper, the *Daily Courant*, in 1702. In the 1990s all the presses and journalists moved to less expensive locations such as Docklands, but the name 'Fleet Street' is still used when referring to the national newspapers.

Cross over to the west side of Farringdon Street, which continues as New Bridge Street, and continue as far as No. 14.

11. BRIDEWELL

Here Henry VIII built the royal palace of Bridewell, named after a holy well nearby which was dedicated to St Bride. There was a bridge across the Fleet at this point

A bust of King Edward VI over the entrance to the former Bridewell Prison

which allowed access to the hospitality of the Blackfriars Monastery on the other side of the river. Henry's son, Edward VI, gave it to the City as a workhouse and prison, and it survived until the 1860s when all the prisoners were transferred to Holloway and the building was demolished. Only the 1802 gatehouse remains, surmounted by a bust of Edward VI. You can also see a plaque with a brief description of its history.

Cross New Bridge Street by the traffic lights and carry on to The Black Friar pub.

12. THE BLACK FRIAR

This is the site of Blackfriars Monastery, founded in the thirteenth century by the Dominicans. Henry VIII entertained the Emperor Charles V here on his visit in 1525, but he dissolved the monastery shortly afterwards in 1538 and nothing remains except a piece of its wall in New Ireland Yard, a short walk past the back of the pub. The pub itself was built in 1900 in the art nouveau style. The statue of a portly friar implies that good food and drink are still available here, thus keeping up the hospitable reputation of the former monastery. You can see a mosaic above the pub entrance, showing two friars catching a plump salmon in the river flowing past their monastery.

Go down the steps to the subway and keep on to exit 6. Here you emerge from under the bridge on to the Thames Path. Walk a few metres in an easterly direction until you reach the top of a ladder by the river wall.

13. FLEET MOUTH

If you look over the river wall, you can see the ladder descending to the riverbed. At the bottom when the tide is out you can see an arch where the culverted River Fleet flows into the Thames. In fact water only flows after heavy rain, when unfortunately a certain amount of pollution accompanies it.

Here you can admire the road bridge, with its five

wrought iron arches on granite piers, built by Joseph Cubitt. The abutments supporting the bridge have carved semicircular projecting balustrades on top, resembling pulpits. This was done at the request of Queen Victoria to remind people of the former monastery.

Just downstream you can see the remaining cast-iron columns of the first Blackfriars Railway Bridge built in 1864, also by Joseph Cubitt. The bridge itself was removed in 1985, as the later railway bridge you can see to the east started taking trains over the river to the new Blackfriars Station. Under the bridge you have a view of the former Bankside Power Station, now housing the Tate Modern Art Gallery.

Return via the subway to Blackfriars Station.

ADDRESSES AND OPENING TIMES

The information below on opening times and admission charges is believed to be correct for the summer of 2004. Most places with free entry are grateful for a donation. Some places close or have different opening times during the winter season. It is recommended that you phone in advance to check the current position and for any family discounts. Please note that many places have a latest admission time which is usually an hour before closure.

BA LONDON EYE
Riverside Building, Westminster Bridge Road, London SE1 7PB
Tel: 0870 500 0600
Open: Daily 9.30 a.m.–8 p.m.
Admission: Adult £11.50, Concessions £10.50, Child £6

BANQUETING HOUSE
Whitehall, London SW1A 2ER
Tel: 020 7930 4179
Open: Mon–Sat 10 a.m.–5 p.m. (but check, as closed for special events)
Admission: Adult £4, Concessions £3, Child £2.60

BOSTON MANOR
Boston Manor Road, Brentford, Middx TW8 9JX
Tel: 0845 456 2800
Open: Sat/Sun/Bank Holidays 2.30 p.m.–5 p.m.
Entry free

BRUNEL ENGINE HOUSE
Railway Avenue, London SE16 4LF
Tel: 020 7231 3840
Open: Sat/Sun 1 p.m.–5 p.m.
Admission: Adult £2, Concessions £1

BURGH HOUSE
New End Square, Hampstead, London NW3 ILT
Tel: 020 7431 0144
Open: Wed–Sun 12 p.m.–5 p.m., Bank Holidays
2 p.m.–5 p.m.
Entry free

CASCADES ART GALLERY
The Pool of Little Venice, Blomfield Road, London
W9 2PA
Tel: 020 7289 7050
Open: Phone for current times
Entry free

CHISWICK HOUSE
Burlington Lane, London W4 2RP
Tel: 020 8995 0508
Open: Wed–Sun 10 a.m.–6 p.m., Sat close 2 p.m.
Admission: Adult £3.50, Concessions £3, Child £2

CLERK'S WELL
14–16 Farringdon Lane, London EC1
Tel: 020 7527 7960
Open: By appointment
Entry free

CLINK PRISON MUSEUM
Soho Wharf, 1 Clink Street, London SE1 9DG
Tel: 020 7378 1338
Open: Daily 10 a.m.–9 p.m.
Admission: Adult £4, Concessions £3, Child £3

CUTTY SARK
King William Walk, Greenwich, London SE10 9HT
Tel: 020 8858 3445
Open: Daily 10 a.m.–6 p.m.
Admission: Adult £3.95, Concessions £2.95, Child £2.95

DESIGN MUSEUM
28 Shad Thames, London SE1 2YD
Tel: 020 7940 8790
Open: Daily 10 a.m.–5.45 p.m.
Admission: Adult £6, Concessions £4, Child £4

FULLER'S GRIFFIN BREWERY TOURS
Chiswick, London W4 2QB
Tel: 020 8996 2063
Open: Tours Mon/Wed/Thu/Fri at 11 a.m., 12 p.m.,
1 p.m., 2 p.m. Phone to book
Admission: £5

HMS *BELFAST*
Morgans Lane, Tooley Street, London SE1 2JH
Tel: 020 7940 6300
Open: Daily 10 a.m.–6 p.m.
Admission: Adult £6, Concessions £4.40, Child free

HOGARTH'S HOUSE
Hogarth Lane, Great West Road, London W4 2QN.
Tel: 020 8994 6757.
Open: Tue–Fri 1 p.m.–5 p.m., Sat–Sun and Bank
Holidays 1 p.m.–6 p.m.
Entry free, but suggested donation £2

JEWEL TOWER
Westminster, London SW1P 3JY
Tel: 020 7222 2219
Open: Daily 10 a.m.–6 p.m.
Admission: Adult £2, Concessions £1.50, Child £1

KEATS HOUSE
Wentworth Place, Keats Grove, London NW3 2RR
Tel: 020 7435 2062
Open: Tue–Sun 12 p.m.–5 p.m.
Admission: Adult £3, Concessions £1.50, Child free

KELMSCOTT HOUSE
26 Upper Mall, Hammersmith, London W6 9TA
Tel: 020 8741 3735
Open: Thurs and Sat 2 p.m.–5 p.m.
Entry free

KEW BRIDGE STEAM MUSEUM
Green Dragon Lane, Brentford, Middx TW8 0EN
Tel: 020 8568 4757
Open: Daily and Bank Holidays 11 a.m.–5 p.m.
Admission: Adult £4.60, Concessions £3.70, Child
£2.50, free after 4 p.m.

KEW GARDENS
Kew, Richmond, Surrey TW9 3AB
Tel: 020 8332 5614
Open: Daily 9.30 a.m. until sunset
Admission: Adult £7.50, Concessions £5.50, Child free

LONDON ZOO
Regent's Park, London NW1 4RY
Tel: 020 7449 6260
Open: Daily 10 a.m.–5.30 p.m.
Admission: Adult £12, Concessions £10.20, Child £9

MIDDLE TEMPLE HALL
Middle Temple Lane, London EC4
Tel: 020 7427 4800
Open: Phone for latest information
Entry free

MONUMENT
Monument Street, London EC3 8AH
Tel: 020 7626 2717
Open: Daily 9.30 a.m.–5 p.m.
Admission: Adult £2, Child £1

MOUNT PLEASANT SORTING OFFICE
Farringdon Road, London EC1
Tel: 020 7239 2331
Open: By appointment. Contact the Tour Manager
Entry free

MUSEUM IN DOCKLANDS
No.1 Warehouse, West India Quay, Hertsmere Road,
London E14 4AL
Tel: 0870 444 3856
Open: Daily 10 a.m.–6 p.m.
Admission: Adult £5, Concessions £3, Students/Under-
16 free

MUSEUM OF GARDEN HISTORY
Lambeth Palace Road, London SE1 7LB
Tel: 020 7401 8865
Open: Daily 10.30 a.m.–5 p.m.
Suggested donation: Adult £2.50, Concession £2

NATIONAL MARITIME MUSEUM, ROYAL OBSERVATORY AND QUEEN'S HOUSE
Greenwich, London SE10 9NF
Tel: 020 8858 4422. Information line 020 8312 6565
Open: Daily 10 a.m.–5 p.m.
Entry free

NORTH WOOLWICH RAILWAY MUSEUM
Pier Road, North Woolwich, London E16 2JJ
Tel: 020 7474 7244
Open: Sat/Sun 1 p.m.–5 p.m.
Entry free

OLD OPERATING THEATRE
9a St Thomas Street, London SE1 9RY
Tel: 020 7955 4791
Open: Daily 10.30 a.m.–5 p.m.
Admission: Adult £4, Concession £3, Child £2.50

PALACE OF WESTMINSTER
Information regarding tours is constantly changing.
Phone 020 7219 3000 for the current situation.

PUBLIC RECORD OFFICE
Kew, Richmond, Surrey TW9 4DU
Tel: 020 8876 3444
Open: Mon/Wed/Fri 9.30 a.m.–5 p.m., Tue 10 a.m.–
7 p.m., Thu 9 a.m.–7 p.m., Sat 9.30 a.m.–5 p.m.
Entry free

RICHMOND MUSEUM
Old Town Hall, Whittaker Avenue, Richmond, Surrey
TW9 1TP
Tel: 020 8332 1141
Open: Tue–Sat 11 a.m.–5 p.m., Sun 1 p.m.–4 p.m.
Admission: Adult £2, Concessions £1, Child free

ROYAL NAVAL COLLEGE (PAINTED HALL AND CHAPEL)
Greenwich, London SE10
Tel: 020 8269 4747
Open: Mon–Sat 10 a.m.–5 p.m., Sun 12.30 p.m.–5 p.m.
Entry free

SHAKESPEARE'S GLOBE EXHIBITION
New Globe Walk, Bankside, London SE1 9DT
Tel: 020 7902 1500
Open: Daily 10 a.m.–5 p.m.
Admission: Adult £8, Concessions £6.50, Child £5

SOMERSET HOUSE
Strand, London WC2R 1LA
Tel: 020 7845 4600
Open: Daily 10 a.m.–6 p.m.
Free entry to building
Gilbert Collection Admission: Adult £5, Concessions £4,
Student/Under-18 free
Courtauld Institute Gallery Admission: Adult £5,
Concessions £4, Student/Under-18 free
Hermitage Rooms Admission: Adult £6, Concessions £4,
Child free

ST ETHELDREDA'S
14 Ely Place, London EC1N 6RY
Tel: 020 7405 1061
Open: Daily except during church services. Phone for
times
Entry free

ST MARY'S, ROTHERHITHE
St Marychurch Street, London SE16 4HY
Tel: 020 7231 2465
Open: 8 a.m.–6 p.m. Sunday service 9.30 a.m., 6 p.m.
Entry free

ST NICHOLAS CHURCH, CHISWICK
The Vicarage, Chiswick Mall, London W4 2PJ
Tel: 020 8995 4717
Open: Tue/Thu mornings
Entry free

ST PANCRAS OLD CHURCH
Pancras Road, London NW1
Tel: 020 7387 7301
Open: By appointment

SYON HOUSE AND PARK
Syon Park, Brentford, Middx TW6 8JF
Tel: 020 8560 0881
Open: Wed, Thu, Sun, Bank Holidays 11 a.m.–5 p.m.
Admission: Adult £6.95, Concessions £5.95, Child £5.95

TATE MODERN ART GALLERY
Bankside, London SE1 9TG
Tel: 020 7887 8000
Open: Mon–Thu 10 a.m.–6 p.m., Fri–Sun 10 a.m.–
10 p.m.
Entry free. Admission charges for special exhibitions

TEMPLE CHURCH
Inner Temple Treasury Office, London EC4
Tel: 020 7797 8250
Open: Phone for latest information
Entry free

TOWER BRIDGE EXPERIENCE MUSEUM
Tower Bridge, London SE1 2UP
Tel: 020 7403 3761
Open: Daily 9.30 a.m.–6 p.m.
Admission: Adult £4.50, Concessions £3, Child £3

TOWER OF LONDON
Tower Hill, London EC3N 4AB
Tel: 020 7709 0765
Open: Mon–Sat 9 a.m –6 p.m., Sun 10 a.m.–6 p.m.
Admission: Adult £13.50, Concessions £10.50, Child £9

VINOPOLIS
1 Bank End, London SE1 9BU
Tel: 0870 241 4040
Open: Mon/Fri/Sat 11 a.m.–9 p.m., Tue/Wed/Thu/Sun 11 a.m.–6 p.m.
Admission: Fri–Mon Adult £12.50, Concessions £11.50
Tue–Thu Adult £11, Concessions £10

WESTMINSTER ABBEY
Broad Sanctuary, London SW1P 3PA
Tel: 020 7222 5152
Open: Mon–Fri 9.30 a.m.–5.45 p.m., Sat 9.30 a.m.–3.45 p.m.
Admission: Adult £6, Concessions £4, Child £4, Under-11 free

WESTMINSTER ABBEY CHAPTER HOUSE AND PYX CHAMBER
East Cloisters, London SW1P 3PE
Tel: 020 7222 5897
Open: Daily 9 a.m.–5 p.m.
Admission: Adult £2.50, Concessions £1.90, Child £1.30

FURTHER READING

There are hundreds of books written about London and its rivers, canals and docks. The following list of books relevant to the walks is by no means exhaustive. Many places issue guidebooks, but unfortunately there are too many to include here. The starting point for any student of London is *The London Encyclopaedia*. The other books listed have also been helpful in my researches and provide more detailed information about the areas covered by the walks than I have been able to include here.

Aslet, Clive, *The Story of Greenwich*, Fourth Estate, London, 1999

Barton, Nicholas, *The Lost Rivers of London*, Historical Publications, London, 1992

Blomfield, David, *Kew Past*, Phillimore & Co. Ltd, Chichester, 1994

Bradley, S. and Pevsner, N., *London I: The City of London*, Penguin, London, 1997

Chaplin, Peter, *The Thames from Source to Tideway*, Whittet Books Ltd, Ipswich, 1988

Clegg, Gillian, *Chiswick Past*, Historical Publications, London, 1995

Cloake, John, *Richmond Past*, Historical Publications, London, 1998

Clout, H., *The Times London History Atlas,* Times Books, London, 1995

Denny, Barbara, *Hammersmith and Shepherds Bush Past*, Historical Publications, London, 1995

Duncan, Andrew, *Secret London*, New Holland Publishers, London, 1995

Ebel, S. and Impey, D., *Guide to London's Riverside, Hampton Court to Greenwich*, Constable and Company Ltd, London, 1985

Essex-Lopresti, Michael, *Exploring the Regent's Canal*, Brewin Books, Midlands, 1987

Farmer, Alan, *Hampstead Heath*, Historical Publications, London, 1996

Hibbert, Christopher, *London: The Biography of a City*, Penguin Books, London, 1980

Humphrey, Stephen, *The Story of Rotherhithe*, London Borough of Southwark, London, 1997

Leapman, Michael, *London's River*, Pavilion Books Ltd, London, 1991

Royal River, Bloomsbury, London, 1985

Trench, R. and Hillman, E., *London under London*, John Murray, London, 1985

Weightman, Gavin, *London River*, Collins and Brown, London, 1990

Weinreb, B. and Hibbert, C., *The London Encyclopaedia*, Macmillan, London, 1995

INDEX